ST. LOUIS at WAR

ST. LOUIS at WAR

THE STORY OF A CITY
1941 — 1945

Betty Burnett

The Patrice Press
St. Louis, Mo.

Library of Congress
Cataloging In Publication Data

Burnett, Betty, 1940-

   Includes index.
   1. World War, 1939-1945 — Missouri — St. Louis.
2. St. Louis (Mo.) — History.   I. Title.
II. Title; Saint Louis at war.
D769.85.M81S253 1987   977.8´66042   87-15591
ISBN 0-935284-52-4

The Patrice Press
1701 S. Eighth St. Louis MO 63104

Printed in the United States of America

To the ingenuity, grit, and belief in tomorrow
that won the war
and to my parents who 'kept 'em rolling'

CONTENTS

FOREWORD

EVERY ST. LOUISAN, every American, should be proud of the accomplishments made by the people of our great city as detailed by Dr. Betty Burnett in her superb contribution about the efforts made by the companies and all the people of our community. Those of us who were involved can take special pride in this accounting of our part of the effort which resulted in the preservation of freedom for the United States and the entire free world. Let's hope that as many people as possible read *St. Louis at War,* a fascinating history which none of us could ever forget.

— Stuart Symington
May 1987

Stuart Symington was president of Emerson Electric Company during World War II.

INTRODUCTION

TRYING TO FIND INFORMATION on St. Louis industries during
World War II was a challenge. Many of those active in business and
industry during the war years have retired and left the area. In their
stead are young people who don't remember the frantic mobilization of
the period — their attention is on the future rather than on the past.
Many businesses of the 1940s have disappeared or have been merged
into conglomerates.

Several companies were especially helpful in discussing their role
during the war. Among them are Nooter Corporation, Koken Industries, Duke Manufacturing Company, Stupp Brothers Bridge and
Iron Company, McQuay-Norris, Jackes Evans Manufacturing Company, Nixdorf Krein Industries, Essmueller Machine Company, and
Angelica Uniform Group.

Many area librarians and archivists helped find information for the
book. I appreciate very much the time and attention given me by John
Hoover and Charles Brown at the Mercantile Library, Anne Kinney
and Kenn Thomas at the Western Historical Manuscripts Collection at
UMSL, Stephanie Klein at Missouri Historical Society, Noel C.
Holobeck at the St. Louis Public Library, and Beryl Manne, archivist
at Olin Library, Washington University.

Finding good photographs to illustrate the book was even more of a
problem than finding facts. Most of the photos in this book were copied
by Gregory M. Franzwa, director of the Patrice Press, from
newspapers (primarily the *Globe-Democrat)* at the Mercantile Library.

The quality is not as good as we would like. The greatest disappointment in the preparation of this book was learning that the photos taken during the war years by *Star-Times* and *Post-Dispatch* photographers had been destroyed. Several photographs were supplied by those responding to an appeal in the *Second Fifty Forum*.

Bob Hardy and Grant Horton of KMOX radio put me in touch with several people in the area who had participated in the mobilization for the war. I especially thank Lilian Holcomb for her invaluable recollections. The story about Otto Dingledein came from Harlow Donovan. Al Bell at AVSCOM/TROSCOM (once U.S. Cartridge) added information and photographs on that important plant.

Thanks also goes to Oscar W. Rexford and my father, Frederick O. Detweiler, for reading the manuscript and offering important suggestions for improving it. Murry Morose, an expert on military hardware, clarified many confusing points about artillery and other armaments. My son, Michael, gave me much encouragement, for which I am very grateful. Henry Stahr copied most of the photos on short notice and although he had to work with very poor prints, produced some very fine pictures. John Ahearn created the powerful illustration for the cover from a mass of material and a hundred suggestions. Finally I thank the team at Patrice Press — especially Brenda Record — for their patience, good humor, and hard work in getting this book out.

I would like to add to the list of area companies which converted to defense work that I compiled (see Appendix). Any information should be sent to The Patrice Press, 1701 S. Eighth Street, St. Louis MO 63104. The generation that worked so hard to win the war should be remembered for its achievements — and that includes making sunglasses for pilots as well as dropping bombs.

My research on the war, although exhilarating, was also sobering.

Whenever I got caught up in the hoopla of bond drives and booming factories, flag-waving and enemy-hating, a visit to the garden of remembrance across from Soldiers' Memorial reminded me: war is hell.

Betty Burnett
May 31, 1987

ST. LOUIS at WAR

THE FIRST WEEK —
DECEMBER 7-14, 1941

ATTACK

THE INTERRUPTION WAS BRIEF. Listeners to KSD's Sunday afternoon program "The University of Chicago Round Table" heard only a terse announcement:

"President Roosevelt has just announced that the Japanese have bombed Hawaii."

That was all. But it was enough to send a rush of anger, a shiver of excitement, and a tremor of fear down Gravois, up Grand, across Natural Bridge, into Florissant farm houses, and out across the Municipal Bridge. As the details of the attack became available, outrage spread across the country like a great, furious thunderstorm: Nineteen U.S. ships had been sunk and 2,300 American lives had been lost.

Within twenty-four hours of the first announcement of the attack the United States was at war with Japan. In another four days war had been declared on Germany and Italy.

Whatever else had been on the agenda for the next four years disappeared overnight. There was only one item on the list now: Victory. Out of closets, basements, and attics came forgotten courage, perseverance, ingenuity, and that most important ingredient — a sense of humor. It was time to get cracking. Look out, Tojo. Look out, Hitler. St. Louis was at war.

The immediate fear was that the attack would spread inland, that enemy agents were already in position to disrupt vital services, throwing the country into confusion and citizens into a panic. Almost immediately after the attack on Pearl Harbor was announced, troops with fixed bayonets were dispatched to guard the ammunition plant at Goodfellow and Bircher, 150 fully-armed soldiers surrounded Lambert

Field and the Curtiss-Wright aircraft plant, and police were sent to watch the Daniel Boone, Eads, and Chain of Rocks bridges. Across the river a platoon of soldiers patrolled Union Electric's Venice and Cahokia plants. Workers going to the TNT factory at Weldon Springs on Monday morning, December 8, were checked to make certain there were no saboteurs among them.

Within a few days Missouri Governor Forrest C. Donnell announced that the army could guard only four strategic bridges in the state and only the Daniel Boone in the St. Louis area. That left 588 Missouri bridges unprotected. Civil Defense coordinator Col. Harry D. McBride hoped that police and firemen could take over. The army also began withdrawing its troops from protecting area defense plants — the men were needed elsewhere.

Before a week had passed, twenty aliens — nineteen Germans and one Italian — were labeled "dangerous" and jailed. Thirty- three Japanese residents were interrogated by the police, including the owner of the Tokyo Restaurant, but they were not found to be a threat. All property owned by Japanese and Koreans was seized and their assets frozen. The Kobe Restaurant (919 Market), Oriental Kitchen (3189 S. Grand) and Oriental Food Supply (3950 Delmar) were closed and guarded around the clock. The Kobe, incidentally, was discovered to be a bookie joint, but no evidence of a link to Japan was found.

At the Bridle Spur Hunt Club on Lindbergh Boulevard, manager Tetsu Uyeda was arrested by the FBI as a suspected spy. He was, admittedly, an agent of the Japanese Tourist Bureau, but he had lived in the United States since 1904 and in St. Louis since 1912. His wife was American-born and their daughter was married to band leader Al Tucker. When he was arrested, Uyeda murmured sadly, "My happy days are ended; too bad, too bad." It seemed incredible to imagine that his loyalty to the emperor superceded that to his adopted home, yet it was difficult to know whom to trust.

When the armed forces recruiting offices at the Federal Building on Market Street opened on December 8, lines of hopeful enlistees were waiting. Capt. E. N. Frakes said it was a "big day" for the army. Across the nation millions of men were needed at once and draft boards were not yet well enough organized to respond quickly. America had an urgent need especially for pilots and aviation cadets. Only 3,600 combat planes were available in December 1941; the U.S. needed ten times that many. A Curtiss-Wright spokesman said that within a month, the company "will be producing so many planes we won't know where to put them" — AT-9 trainers, C-46 cargo transports, and navy SNC-1 combat trainers.

At the office of the First Missouri Infantry, Missouri State Guard, at 403 Olive, Col. Ethan A. H. Shepley was flooded with applicants, so

Eager young men jammed the navy's recruiting office on December 8, 1941.

many that he had to close the office until he could get help with the paper work. Maj. William B. Robertson, president of Robertson Aircraft Corporation, was named commander of the Missouri wing of the Civil Air Patrol by Fiorella H. La Guardia, national Civilian Defense chief. Robertson vowed to maintain a patrol of private planes in Missouri "to prevent unauthorized private flights over defense areas." However, almost all private planes were sent either east or west to patrol the coasts.

All furloughs were canceled for those already in the military. Soldiers hurried back to Jefferson Barracks, Scott Field, and Fort Leonard Wood. The National Guard and reserves were called up. Sentries at Jefferson Barracks were ordered to fire at persons who failed to obey the command to halt. At 4 A.M. on December 8 nervous guards shot several times at a milk truck that refused to stop at the gate. No one was injured.

As lines continued to grow at recruiting offices, it became obvious that men couldn't both serve abroad and produce defense materiel at home. Women were called to pitch in. They came running. Only three days after Pearl Harbor it was announced that five women would be trained in aeronautics "to fit them for minor positions now held by men" at the aviation plants.

Because of Lend-Lease, the U.S. had been producing war materiel for Great Britain since March 1941. Curtiss-Wright and Emerson

Emerson Electric's aircraft gun turret plant, the largest such plant in the world, was still under construction in December 1941.

Electric were among the companies which began gearing up production for the Allies. With the announcement of war, they immediately began hiring more workers. Emerson Electric had won a contract to produce parts for airplane turrets. Although the new plant was only twenty percent completed in December 1941, employees made their way through the construction and set to work.

St. Louis was in a mood to work — and to fight. Traffic patrolman Ed Boehmer summed up the feeling of urgency: "Let's go get them and put in everything we've got. Spare nothing." And newsboy Charles Chervitz said, "There are no more minorities. We're all united now and we'll beat the Axis powers."

And the city was almost united. On the Hill, the Italian community lined up for the Allied cause as soon as Il Duce declared war on America. Joseph Riggio of Riggio Realty said, "All Italian people here . . . are 100 percent for the United States." Joseph Volpi, head of Volpi and Co., was buying as many defense bonds as he could afford. But there was sorrow too. Rev. Fiorenzo Lupo, pastor of St. Ambrosius Italian Catholic Church, deeply regretted the war. "I am very sorry," he told reporters. And customers looked with suspicion at restaurant owner Joe Garavelli, who had once been decorated by the Italian government.

The fear of sabotage haunted the city. Mayor William Dee Becker decided to have all city employees fingerprinted as a precaution. St. Louisans also feared that Japan would stage a "hit and run" air raid and the city was in no way prepared. In the spring of 1941, then-Mayor Bernard F. Dickmann had suggested that the city begin preparing a civil defense program, but by December, the program was still only a vague plan.

"Be calm and be patient," Colonel McBride told uneasy citizens. But organizing the defense of a major metropolitan area was not something that could be done in a day or two. St. Louis didn't even have sirens to warn people of an impending air raid. It needed air raid wardens (one for every 500 people was recommended), rescue squads, evacuation routes, first-aid facilities, alternate transportation and

Three hundred and fifty students from Howard elementary school marched to the Northwest National Bank on December 10, 1941, to buy defense stamps.

power sources, repair units, and firefighters.

Again St. Louisans rolled up their sleeves and lined up to help. Within a week the city had 850 volunteer firefighters. Fifty-one auxilary fire companies were being formed and the call went out to find some 6,000 fire and air raid wardens. Max Doyne, director of public utilities, asked for an ''army of volunteers'' to enforce blackouts, patrol power stations, and help maintain communications in case of attack. Charles H. Ellaby, president of the board of the Public Service Company, was put in charge of locating air raid shelters, planning a mass evacuation, organizing rescue parties, distributing gas masks, and providing food and shelter for those bombed out. He looked for volunteers too. Others came forward. Four hundred people had donated blood to the American Red Cross blood bank by December 9. Hundreds of women volunteered to be trained as nurses aides to replace nurses who had responded to the War Department's call for help.

If patriotism hadn't been stirred enough by December 10, it was that night in a giant ''It's Fun to Be Free'' rally held at the Municipal (now Kiel) Auditorium. Harry Hall Knight had organized the rally long before the Pearl Harbor attack in an attempt to get St. Louisans in-

"Goodbye, Daddy. Come home soon."

terested in preparedness. He had no trouble in raising a crowd — over 9,000 people attended to watch a review written by Ben Hecht and Charles MacArthur. Burgess Meredith acted as emcee and the cast included Melvyn Douglas, Linda Darnell, Rita Hayworth, Humphrey Bogart, and Phil Silvers, all leading Hollywood stars.

As stirring as the music was and as exciting as it was to see the stars perform, the real highlight of the evening came when Sgt. Alvin C. York, much-decorated hero of the Allied Expeditionary Force in World War I, stepped onto the stage. "Our password," he said, "is 'On To Tokyo!' and we'll get 'em anywhere we find 'em." The crowd cheered. Coincidentally, the film *Sergeant York,* with Gary Cooper, was playing at the Shady Oak and the Hi-Pointe.

One way to "get 'em" was in the pocketbook. On December 10 local chapters of the American Federation of Labor voted to patrol the stores in East St. Louis and to throw out into the street any goods they found that had been made in Japan, Italy, or Germany. A day later, the Central Trades and Labor Union supervised a bonfire in a vacant lot where Christmas decorations made in Japan were burned. The large crowd cheered as it watched red paper bells and Santa Clauses go up in flames.

Newspaper editorials counseled using self-control to keep from getting carried away by anger and fear. "Let us all strive to keep our heads," urged the *Star-Times.* But truck driver John Bronson had another idea. "They asked for it; now they'll get it," he said. ("They Asked For It" was also the name of a hastily-written popular song; it died a merciful death, along with "You're a Sap, Mr. Jap.")

After a week at war, St. Louis was still in a turmoil. Its young people were preparing to fight half a world away. Its economy was quickly becoming dependent on defense contracts. Its citizens nervously watched the skies and each other for signs of disloyalty. The whole world had turned upside down. As *Star-Times* columnist Walter Kiernan wrote, "There was no place in our planned lives for a war." Nonetheless, war had come.

THE FIRST YEAR — 1942
MOBILIZATION

WAR HAD COME THROUGH THE BACK DOOR while the family was upstairs wrapping Christmas presents. No one was ready. But the shock and confusion that followed Pearl Harbor did not last long. The fastest, greatest mobilization the world has ever seen began. On January 7, 1942, President Franklin D. Roosevelt said, "Let no man say it cannot be done. It must be done." And it was done, because no one took the time to doubt.

The moment war was declared, the army announced that it needed five million men in uniform. Another million were needed for the Army Air Corps, the navy and the marines. Together, the armed forces made an urgent plea for 20,000 antiaircraft guns, 45,000 tanks and 60,000 planes. Every ounce of available metal had to go into making weapons, ships, and planes. Congress appropriated $71 billion for the war effort and the work began. (The amount was astronomical in the days when ten cents bought a loaf of bread and the average wage was sixty cents an hour.)

In St. Louis, as the city marshaled its forces to meet the demands of war, officials tackled problems on several fronts. The defense industries had to expand quickly. After the lean years of the Great Depression, the sight of smoke pouring from factory stacks and the sounds of construction brought thousands of job seekers into the city from outstate Missouri, downstate Illinois, and throughout the South.

Already burdened with too much substandard housing, the city tried to absorb the influx, but crowding became almost intolerable. Schools near defense plants began double sessions, and welfare organizations called attention to the numbers of children left unattended while their parents worked. A whole series of social problems, from a dramatic increase in the cases of venereal disease to sudden tension over racial injustice, began to confound the city.

Pictures of the smoking ruins of Hickam Field at Pearl Harbor were still vivid in everyone's mind when city officials turned to their first priority — mapping a defense of the city in case of attack. Because of the fear of sabotage from within the gates, enemy aliens (Italians, Germans and Japanese) were put under close surveillance.

Very soon after Pearl Harbor it became obvious that America's pantry was almost bare. Crucial goods were already scarce and being used up fast. Almost everyone could see that some form of rationing and recycling was inevitable.

But despite the grim forecast and the relentless anxiety, the mood of the city was almost exuberant. Countless opportunities for mettle-testing lay ahead. Suddenly every person was an important part of the battle, regardless of sex, race, age, education, social class or degree of physical fitness. There was a job for each, a job that could bring victory a little bit closer. Few St. Louisans were found shirking — although there were some — and relatively few were found profiteering, hoarding, chiseling, or grumbling. Almost everyone was eager to join the fight.

Since St. Louis is located in the heart of the nation, over a thousand miles from either coast, the city was not a logical target for an attack by the Axis powers. But logic was not foremost in the minds of Americans after Pearl Harbor. As late as April 1942 Secretary of War Henry L. Stimson declared that an attack on the continental United States was "inevitable" and could occur any time, anywhere. It was best to be ready.

The key targets within the St. Louis metropolitan area were likely to be the three ammunition plants, at Alton, Weldon Spring, and in the city at Goodfellow and Bircher. The airport, railroad depot, bridges, utility companies, and reservoirs were also likely to be hit. At first the army and National Guard were put in charge of protecting these installations, but soon most developed their own security systems.

With a show of pugnacious rhetoric, city aldermen appropriated $50,000 to spend on protection for St. Louis immediately after Pearl Harbor, which included $4,500 for lighting Municipal (now MacArthur) Bridge. Later, when blackouts were ordered, all the lights in the city went out except those which outlined the bridge, making it a superb target.

Rather than preparing for an all-out enemy onslaught, the city decided to prepare for a hit-and-run attack — a blitz of small incendiary bombs — which seemed more likely. Such an attack would not immobilize the city through immediate devastation, but would disrupt it by a series of small fires, broken water mains, and impassable streets.

Activity was intense at Civil Defense headquarters in the Civil Courts building at Eleventh and Market.

Those who had lived through the London blitz were called in for advice. At Stix Baer and Fuller downtown, for instance, a member of the London Auxiliary Fire Service played a recording of an air raid to prepare its 2,000 employees for the terrifying sounds of an attack. He told them the best way to handle the inevitable panicky crowds once the bombs started falling. "It is your duty to yourselves and to your customers to stay by your station," he said.

Col. Harry D. McBride had been given the responsibility in the fall of 1941 to organize the city-wide civil defense operation. He set up headquarters in the most bomb-proof building in town, the Civil Courts building, and gathered around him every means of communication then known except television — two-way radios, police radios, a fire department alarm system, multiple telephone lines with four separate underground wire channels, and messengers who delivered bulletins daily to civil defense outposts.

Armed guards surrounded the communications division. Beyond them was the "heart and nerve center" of headquarters, where McBride met with his function chiefs to plot strategy. Here giant maps of the city were marked off into zones. Police, fire, rescue, medical, and repair units were assigned to each zone. A "traffic light" warning system was developed, activated by the presence of enemy planes in the vicinity. If a green light flashed, it meant it was time to run for cover.

The radio was America's lifeline during the war. Soldiers at Forest Park's recreation camp listen intently to the latest war news. It wasn't good.

All of the civil defense units were made up of volunteers — McBride wanted over 100,000 of them — who were trained at night classes in first aid, crowd control, airplane recognition, and restoring disrupted utilities. One of the assignments given trainees was to sniff a variety of gases so they could identify them easily — mustard, lewisite, phosgene, chlorine, and tear gas.

Guy Mullen, who was in charge of the ambulance division, developed a unique plan for training his drivers. He strapped a 16mm movie camera to the front of his car and then drove at 35 MPH from the small arms plant to DePaul Hospital. Drivers watched the resulting film, memorizing the landmarks so they could drive in a blackout if necessary. Mullen also lined up a dozen panel trucks which were specially outfitted with stretchers and transformed into ambulances.

Trying to keep any helpful information from the enemy, the government banned all weather forecasts within the country. One radio announcer describing weather conditions at a December football game was arbitrarily cut off the air. All the St. Louis radio stations voluntarily began self-censorship and dropped talk shows, request lines and other call-in programs in case someone should inadvertently mention something over the air that might help the enemy. If a caller requested "Moon Over Miami," for instance, or "Chattanooga Choo Choo," or "Deep in the Heart of Texas,"an enemy agent could be alerted to a possible attack. Even "I Don't Want to Set the World on Fire" could have a special, sinister meaning for the Axis.

Radio was a lifeline for Americans during the war years. It connected those at home with the terrible and desperate battles in obscure corners of the earth. Americans showed an almost insatiable need for news of the war. Families huddled around large radio consoles in living rooms or small kitchen radios as they ate breakfast, listening for the words that would mean a son or a neighbor or a brother was safe. At first the news was heavily censored and details of battles were sketchy.

"Somewhere in the Pacific," the destination for millions of sailors, navy pilots, seabees, soldiers, and marines, covered the area from Umak in the Aleutian Islands to Auckland, New Zealand, from Borneo to Honolulu. Throughout 1942 and 1943 St. Louisans anxiously studied maps published in the newspapers and sought out globes at the library for the location of unfamiliar namess: Luzon, Corregidor, Tarawa, Port Moresby, Guam, Midway, Wake, Sevastopol, El Alamein, Tobruk, Bizerte, and the Kasserine Pass. Newsreel footage of troops was carefully scrutinized for a familiar face, for a sign that he was still safe, wherever he was.

The abrupt cessation of weather forecasts in December 1941 meant that no one was allowed to predict if there would be snow for Christmas that year. Whether or not Christmas Eve would be a "midnight clear" was a military secret. Santa Claus was expressly forbidden to fly in the northeast under threat of being shot down. Five weeks later, on February 2, news of the presence (or absence) of the groundhog's shadow was also blocked by the censor.

St. Louisans became so adept at keeping silent about war conditions that when a newspaper reporter monitored fifty conversations throughout the city in February 1942, he heard only two references to the war. The rest of the conversations were about valentines, new hats and office politics. A pleased St. Louisan wrote a letter to the editor pointing out that if the reporter had been a foreign agent, "he wouldn't have learned much."

But the plans for the defense of the city were anything but secret. Both city and county officials publicized the details of their organizations and accepted anyone who volunteered. Volunteers came from all parts of the metropolitan area, from every socio-economic status and educational level. Their ages ranged from fifteen to seventy. Their attitude, said the *Star-Times,* was a determined "we've got to do what we can."

John W. Shocklee, father of ten children and an employee of the St. Louis Public Service Company, volunteered because he wanted his children "to have the same freedom and the same opportunity that I have had in this country." Mrs. Jessie Kriz, a nurse who had served in World War I, said she stepped forward simply because she was an

American. Raymond Parsons, a blind braille proofreader, said he just wanted to do his part.

One of the first to sign up as an air raid warden was August A. Busch, Jr. A number of Sacred Heart nuns graduated from the first OCD training as qualified air raid wardens. Over five hundred nuns, representing fifty-two religious orders and 152 institutions, eventually completed training as wardens. Archbishop John J. Glennon told a group of them on their graduation, "neither our religion nor our cloth can expect any quarter from Hitler."

Four thousand employees of Southwestern Bell, 3,200 from Union Electric and Laclede Gas, and 3,400 postal employees signed up for civil defense duties. The Jewish People's Committee and Italian-American organiza-

Archbishop John J. Glennon urged members of the St. Louis Archdiocese to support the war effort.

tions volunteered to do what they could. And the Missouri Federation of Women's Clubs substituted learning first aid for listening to book reviews.

Mobilizing the city's fifty-seven first aid posts fell to Dr. E. L. Keys. Each unit was assigned two doctors, two nurses, a medical depot custodian and eight stretcher bearers. By January 12, 1942, 18,741 St. Louisans were enrolled in 710 Red Cross classes. An emergency hospital evacuation plan was worked out which designated nearly 19,000 beds to be set up in hospitals, libraries, auditoriums, city buildings, stores, and school gymnasiums. City medical director Dr. W. E. Hennerich named Jefferson Barracks, Koch Hospital, Veterans Hospital, and Mount St. Rose TB Hospital as evacuation centers for whites, and Homer G. Phillips Hospital, Tandy, Vashon, and Gamble Community Centers as evacuation points for blacks.

The county medical director announced that since beds alone did not make a hospital, those injured in the county should go to bona fide medical institutions only, not community centers. The so- called czar of the county defense system was Charles W. Bolan, advertising manager with Carter Carburetor. When he was heavily criticized for "doing nothing" (only twelve percent of his volunteers had been given

Civil Defense volunteers parade in the late spring of 1942.

any sort of instructions by April), he claimed that he needed time to build a solid structure and was not "slapping together a haphazard organization." Meanwhile, in the city, Democratic committeeman Joseph Darst charged Mayor William Dee Becker's civil defense organization with favoritism, since most of its appointees were, like Becker, Republican.

Once the OCD organization was stable, it began to test its ability to respond to an emergency by holding drills. To launch a campaign making St. Louisans aware of civil defense procedures, a pageant, "St. Louis Prepares," was held at the municipal auditorium in February 1942. Every seat was filled. A massive chorus filled the air with heart-stirring patriotic songs. Helen Hayes, surrounded by soldiers from Scott Field, gave a dramatic reading of "America." Films of the bombing of London brought home the seriousness of the occasion. For the finale, sirens throughout the theater wailed while searchlights played across the audience. On stage, firemen and Red Cross workers demonstrated their response to an air raid.

The city's first blackout was held on March 7. At 7:21 P.M. switches were thrown and 50,000 street lights went out. Light from storefronts and homes was the city's only illumination. At 7:23 the street lights went on again and the test was judged successful. A similar blackout at Lambert Airport a few days later was also well done.

In April East St. Louis staged a fifty-minute surprise blackout. Less

Helen Hayes, backed by a chorus from Scott Air Field, gives a dramatic recitation of "America" at Municipal (Kiel) Auditorium.

than three minutes after the first signal, six hundred volunteer workers had reported for duty. Ambulance sirens sounded continuously in the dark city. A *Star-Times* reporter described it as "darned realistic." The lights went out at 8 P.M. as the reporter was driving through the city. He continued, "I was standing on the running board, my foot on the accelerator, peering out into the blackness. . . . Overhead, there was that drone of the airplane looking for lights. All of a sudden it would swoop down with a terrific roar and cut its motor in and out to warn some violator. It got so you began to listen for the whine of a dropped bomb."

Watching newsreels of attacking planes had prepared St. Louisans for the real thing, so when an unidentified plane flew over Western Cartridge Company in East Alton in February, alert guards raced to defend their country. They fired sixty-two rounds of ammunition into the plane, which turned out to be on a sight-seeing tour. Pilot Delbert Richardson of Collinsville was able to land safely, but one of his passengers was seriously wounded. Other pilots reported being fired upon at Weldon Spring and Valley Park and over the small arms plant at Goodfellow and Bircher.

By April the St. Louis OCD reported that it had enrolled 5,300 air raid wardens, 2,438 auxiliary firemen, 3,090 auxiliary policemen, 450 demolition experts, 4,000 drivers, 461 fire watchers, 3,160 persons able

Civil Defense workers demonstrate how to douse a fire caused by an incendiary bomb during the "St. Louis Prepares" pageant.

to give emergency medical care, 213 nurse's aides, 1,000 road repair workers, 2,900 office workers, 3,705 emergency housing committee members, and 19,834 "others." An additional 52,556 women were in Red Cross training, preparing for OCD service. CD workers had made a survey which identified all sources of water in the area, including wells, swimming pools, ponds, and water tanks, which could be used for fire fighting in an emergency.

City building inspector Albert H. Baum looked over hundreds of buildings and subterranean places before selecting two hundred air raid shelters which could protect 40,000 people, only a fraction of the city's population. Most shelters were labeled with a luminescent red-white-and-blue "S."

Area schools decided to keep children in the school buildings during an attack and weekly air raid drills were held in most school systems. It was hoped that each school would become a "self-contained defense unit." Principals agreed to direct fire fighting and teachers began to learn first aid.

As civilians were preparing for the defense of the city, every branch of the armed forces was receiving a flood of applicants. A training facility for the Coast Guard was located at the foot of Washington Avenue. Across the river at Scott Field, Army Air Corps recruits learned radio operation. At Lambert Field the Naval AirStation ex-

Percy Brown, a guard at Lakeside Airport in Granite City, Illinois, points to a bullet hole in the pilot's seat of a sight-seeing airplane. The plane was fired upon by nervous guards in the restricted zone of Western Cartridge Company in East Alton. A passenger was hit and seriously wounded.

panded, then expanded again to handle its enlistees. In south St. Louis County, Jefferson Barracks processed a steady stream of army draftees and offered basic training to about half of them. Near Rolla, Fort Leonard Wood was home to thousands of soldiers and at Neosho, Camp Crowder housed still more.

Beginning early in February all men between the ages of twenty-one and forty-four were required to register for the draft. Later the age limit was dropped to eighteen. In St. Louis 80,600 men responded to the first call. After they were given numbers, they waited for the "fishbowl lottery" which determined the order of call-up.

Many St. Louisans thought that the first Christmas after Pearl Harbor might be the last merry one in some time, so they decided to celebrate it lavishly. Mirroring the upheaval across the nation, travel to, from, and through St. Louis broke all records since they'd first been kept in 1894. A newspaper reporter described Union Station:

"The cavernous midway, during the peak morning and evening hours is a shifting mass of people — men in civilian clothes, men in uniform, women and children streaming out from long, crowded trains, others hurrying through the gates to outbound trains.

"Red caps weave through the crowds loaded down with beribboned packages as well as luggage. Soldiers are everywhere. Above all the noise and shouting come the clear notes of 'Silent Night, Holy Night' played by a little Salvation Army band."

As 1941 came to an end, crowds in St. Louis increased. A record number of reservations were made for all New Year's Eve celebrations and empty hotel rooms could not be found. Restaurants and bars were jammed, the YMCAs were filled, and stray soldiers found sleeping space in lobbies, on billiard tables at bars, and at the bus station. Most parties boasted red, white, and blue decor and "V-for-Victory" cocktails. When celebrants were not singing "Hi Ho, Hi Ho, We're Off to Tokyo" or "Stars and Stripes Forever," they were dancing the rhumba, forming conga lines, or listening to boogie woogie. Some

Emblem of the Naval Air Station, which was located at Lambert Field until 1943, when it was transferred to NAS at Glenview, Illinois.

NAS St. Louis pilots suit up for winter flights from Lambert Field.

Black GIs camped at Blanchette Park in St. Charles.

Coast Guardsmen demonstrate their response to a smoke screen in a chemical warfare drill.

Temporary quarters for the Coast Guard was at the foot of Market Street.

Mrs. Lilton Murrell tells her husband he's number one — in the ward 17 draft lottery.

Barber Frederick J. Scheltings was #1 in District 8, despite being a ''pre-Pearl Harbor father'' five times over. Children are Donald, Mary Lou, Doris, Allan, and Ruth.

''The best damned radio operators in the world'' were trained at Scott Field.

A military wedding at Jefferson Barracks.

party-goers ended up at late-night movies where they shivered over
Lon Chaney, Jr., in *Wolfman,* or Errol Flynn in *They Died With Their
Boots On,* or wept a little over *How Green Was My Valley.*

The uncertainty, the intensity, the excitement, and the anxiety that
gripped the country in December 1941 led to a sudden marriage boom.
In the month following Pearl Harbor 2,434 marriage licenses were
issued in St. Louis, compared with 1,843 in the month before Pearl
Harbor. Eventually the marriage boom led to a baby boom — a record
of more than twenty births per thousand in 1942 — and to a divorce
boom. In 1941 there was an average of thirty divorces a week in St.
Louis; in 1942 there were thirty a day. Ninety-eight percent of these
divorces were in the "high risk draft group," those between the ages of
twenty and thirty-five years.

One judge attributed the high divorce rate to the fact that more
women were working than ever before and suddenly they could afford
to live alone. Industry looked to women workers first reluctantly and
then eagerly as it tried to respond to the nation's call to arms. Within a
month after Pearl Harbor, more than 600 St. Louis plants had converted from production of civilian goods to war materiel, and production had stepped up as much as 150 percent. Before December 7 St.
Louis firms were receiving about $3,000,000 in new government con-
tracts every month. They received $3,126,000 per week the month
after December 7.

Hadley Vocational School is shown ablaze with lights in 1942. Night classes prepared students for work in the defense industries.

Gearing up for the war had actually begun in 1940, when the Chamber of Commerce initiated a census of manufacturers in the area. Under the leadership of Chamber president Thomas N. Dysart, a detailed survey followed. The results, published in five volumes, listed the machinery, equipment, floor space, and manpower available in each St. Louis factory. Copies of the survey were sent to every one of the 1,100 prime defense contractors in the nation, giving St. Louis at least a six-month jump on other cities.

Also in 1940 the Chamber saw the need to upgrade the skills of workers in the area and began a "training within industry" program in cooperation with several schools — Hadley Vocational, Ranken, Jefferson College of the YMCA, Saint Louis University, Washington University, Alton Vocational School, and Booker T. Washington Technical School. Most of the courses revolved around the burgeoning aviation industry, but many taught generalized production skills.

The preparation began to pay off almost immediately. A $16 million order for training and cargo planes was placed with the Curtiss-Wright aircraft plant here in June 1940. In October construction for a $14 million high-explosives plant was begun on 20,000 acres of land near Weldon Spring. Operated by the Atlas Powder Company, the facility became the nation's largest, eventually producing 800 tons of TNT daily.

On December 14, 1940, almost a full year before Pearl Harbor, a

U.S. Cartridge, the largest such plant in the nation, employed 35,000 St. Louisans at its peak. The plant, located north of Natural Bridge Road (bottom of photo) and east of Goodfellow, stretched for several city blocks.

contract for building a small arms ordnance plant at Goodfellow and Bircher was approved. Ground for the facility was broken on March 28, 1941, and production began seven months later. On Monday morning, December 8, less than twenty-four hours after the attack on Pearl Harbor, the army accepted the plant's first completed order of ammunition. By the first anniversary of Pearl Harbor, U. S. Cartridge (or St. Louis Ordnance, as it was also called) had produced one billion rounds of ammunition — over a thousand cartridges for every American soldier sent overseas. (Ripley's "Believe it or Not" stated in 1945, "It would take 337 years for a soldier firing a Garand at its maximum rate of aimed fire to shoot all of the caliber .30 ammunition produced by St. Louis Ordnance Plant.") The largest plant of its type in the world, St. Louis Ordnance employed about 35,000 workers at its peak, in three shifts, six (sometimes seven) days a week.

Cartridges produced at the plant were of the ball, armor piercing, and tracer types. Powder was stored in half-buried "igloos" several miles from the plant, on land now part of the August A. Busch Memorial Wildlife Area. It was hauled in each day. The bullet's steel core was made at nearby McQuay-Norris Manufacturing Company. Each bullet was described as being "blanked and cupped, then annealed and bunted — foredrawn; then it has its head turned, is annealed again, headed and flattened, reduced, gauged, accepted or rejected." Thousands of rounds of ammunition were tested each day at the plant and at several sites in Tyson Valley, including what later became Lone Elk Park.

Those factories that could build tanks — American Car and Foundry Co. and St. Louis Car Co. — also received healthy contracts before war was declared. Busch-Sulzer Diesel Engine Co., which made engines for minesweepers and patrol boats, began a three-shift, seven-day week on December 8, the day it sent a telegram to Secretary of the Navy Frank Knox saying, "You can count on us in every way."

Before the war ended, over seventy-five percent of St. Louis manufacturers became involved in defense work. (The national average was fifty percent.) The range of articles produced was wide: eighty-eight ordnance items (gun turrets, grenade launchers, torpedoes, howitzer shells, bombs), hundred of items for the quartermaster corps (uniforms, helmets, shoes and boots, K-rations, mess kits, bed rolls), equipment for the Army Signal Corps, the Army Corps of Engineers, the Merchant Marine, the U.S. Navy, and the Coast Guard, thousands of tools and machinery parts, chemicals, and drugs.

Monsanto converted almost totally to war production. It manufactured sulfuric acid for TNT, chlorine gas, and phenol. It also produced phosphorus pentoxide, used for refining aviation gasoline, dinitrochlorobenzine, used in making tetryl for high explosives, nitric acid, and fulminate of mercury primers for small arms ammunition. But perhaps its most lasting contribution to the war effort was the production of sulfa compounds which all but eliminated gangrene, saving both lives and limbs.

In January 1942 an estimated 172,000 people were working in area factories. About 14,000 were added each month throughout the year. (The figures are approximate because the exact numbers were censored.) The great need for workers coupled with the federal government's directive forbidding discrimination in employment, pressed employers into hiring more women, blacks, and handicapped workers than ever before in history.

Soon after war broke out Curtiss-Wright announced that it would train women as riveters, inspectors, and electric assembly workers; it was immediately swamped with applications. U.S. Cartridge agreed to hire 3,000 blacks, although it insisted that separate canteens and cafeterias had to be provided for them. Despite the segregation, Arnold Walker, industrial secretary of the Urban League, said, "This is some of the best news that we who have been working against racial

The Curtiss-Wright aircraft factory near Lambert Field employed over 10,000 workers during the war.

discrimination in defense industries have had.'' For the first time, blacks would be hired as skilled workers at rates comparable to whites.

Not all businesses were booming, however. The production of automobiles, stoves, refrigerators, and small electrical appliances was immediately curtailed. Shortages of materials meant that some industries had to struggle to keep afloat. Candy and soft drink manufacturers were hurt by sugar rationing; vinegar and cider-making companies had to work around the rationing of acetic acid. Firms that made caskets, bed springs, and musical instruments found the metal shortage a disaster. The $1,250,000 cleaning preparations industry in St. Louis was threatened by shortages of glycerine, alcohol, carbon tetrachloride, formaldehyde, and waxes. Printing companies found it impossible to get metallic inks and high-grade paper. And while production at the breweries was at an all-time high, the shortage of metal for cans and of cork for bottlecaps meant that most beer had to be sold in kegs.

Shortages hit consumers as hard as they hit businesses. The first was rubber. The sale of new tires was frozen the week after Pearl Harbor and did not ease for the duration because rubber plantations were in Japanese hands. As soon as the rubber shortage was announced by Leon Henderson, chief of the Office of Price Administration (OPA), sales of golf and tennis balls increased 200 percent in St. Louis. Rubber footwear sold out. Rubber was banned in the manufacture of corsets, girdles, suspenders, bras, and other elastic-supported undergarments, which caused delight, alarm, and a slew of corny jokes.

By the first of the year the St. Louis rationing board had been established to regulate the sale of tires and inner tubes. Edward G.

Platt was appointed administrator. Getting a new tire took endurance. First the old tires were inspected at an authorized service station. Next the hopeful buyer filled out a questionnaire. If the tires were indeed showing their age and the need seemed legitimate, the service station attendant issued a certificate, which the applicant took to the rationing board in the Civil Courts building. After hearing the case, the board decided to give — or more often, not to give — permission to purchase a tire.

The January quota of tires for St. Louis was 2,154 and considerably less for St. Louis County. The reality was that ninety percent of all drivers were unable to obtain new tires. Those who did were designated indispensable; most new tires were for ambulances and other emergency vehicles. Hearses were not allowed new tires, nor were taxis, and only a few were allocated for buses. A physician who was able to obtain four new tires and drove to Colorado for a vacation on them found when he got back to St. Louis that he had to turn them over to the board. "Every time a man goes fishing on a rationed tire, he is violating the law," said state rationing director William H. Bryan.

As tire rationing began, a wave of tire thefts followed. The first weekend that rationing was in effect, twenty-five tires and eleven wheels were stolen. Beaumont High School teacher Irene Gibson walked into her garage one morning to find her car jacked up and stripped of its wheels, tires, and spare. She was not the only one to discover such an unwelcome surprise.

Tire thieves immediately went to the top of the list of rotten criminals. Alderman Claude I. Bakewell called for the stiffest possible penalty for them, up to six months in the workhouse. The maximum penalty for falsifying information to the rationing board was ten years in prison and $10,000 in fines. A black market in tires flourished, but many of the tires sold this way had been salvaged from junk yards and were all but worthless. Tire retread shops went on a 24-hour day and a seven-day week and raised their prices by twenty-five percent, but still couldn't keep up with the demand.

The May 18 *Star Times* told a pathetic story about a serviceman who only wanted to visit his hometown.

Everywhere This Soldier Went,
His Tires Were Sure To Blow

Staff Sergt. John L. Baldini of Jefferson Barracks wants to whip the Japs right now — so we can get rubber again.

Hark to his tale of tire woes. En route in his car to his

home at Bloomington, Ill., happy possessor of a three-day pass, Baldini got as far as White Hall, Ill., when a rear tire blew out. He could get no replacement, so he continued with a White Hall friend who had offered to drive him the rest of the way. But a tire on the friend's car blew out almost immediately.

So Baldini boarded a bus and got to Bloomington — after a pause while the bus driver changed a flat tire. His family offered to drive him and a fairly new tire to White Hall to pick up his abandoned car. The family car had a blowout on the way. And as he drove up to headquarters, his leave over, he had, yes, another flat tire.

To save tires, stores, laundries, and dairies curtailed home deliveries. County high schools dropped their spring schedules for baseball, track and field, and golf because they didn't have the tires to travel. As many as 60,000 cars were parked in garages as their owners began to use public transportation. The already overburdened Public Service transit system struggled to adapt to the increasing number of riders. Washington Avenue downtown became a tangle of streetcars, buses, pedestrians, and cars.

A unique feature of St. Louis traffic was the "service car," an automobile that followed the bus line and picked up riders for a modest fee. Much cheaper than taxis and faster than buses, service cars were more popular with riders than with city officials, who accused them of careless driving as they whipped in and out of traffic looking for passengers. Because service cars enjoyed the patronage of certain aldermen, they were not required to meet the regulations that other public vehicles met, and they were not insured.

When gas rationing began in the fall of 1942, the strain on public transportation increased. Several 1928 double-decker buses were brought out of storage and used during rush hour. They were retired for good after only a few months in service — no one wanted to risk riding in them. An innovation designed to shoehorn eighty-eight instead of fifty-six riders onto a bus was the "stand-sit,"a sort-of seat that the rider leaned against. One rider said, "Now I know how a sardine feels."

New cars were also rationed and practically impossible to find because automobile manufacturers had turned to producing trucks, jeeps, and tanks. (Later, cars *were* impossible to find.) In February twenty-six new cars were released for St. Louis. Vladimir Golschmann, conductor of the St. Louis Symphony Orchestra, was

The sugar shortage was taken in stride by most St. Louisans. Here a housewife is turning in her extra sugar, probably a staged event. Few homes had a surplus.

one of the recipients. For March, April, and May combined, the car quota for St. Louis was 785; for St. Louis County it was 291. The car dealers who survived turned to servicing, rather than selling, cars and swallowed the loss of their occupation with a show of pragmatic patriotism.

By the end of January the unofficial word was that sugar would be the next product to be rationed. St. Louisans went on a "mild buying spree," which could almost be described as hoarding, as thousands of pounds of sugar were bought and put away for future use.

By the time sugar rationing began in May, St. Louisans had hardened themselves to the loss. Members of the Women's Advertising Club insisted, "Don't call me sugar — it's not patriotic!" and homemakers gamely lined up at elementary schools to get war ration books. Each family member was issued a book, regardless of age, and was alloted one pound of sugar each two weeks.

Restaurants tried different ways of rationing sugar to customers. The Senate Restaurant downtown hid its sugar bowls and made people ask for them. Some restaurants allowed one teaspoon per customer, others sparingly distributed sugar packets or cubes. Diners who wanted more than one cup of coffee (or one teaspoonful of sugar) began carrying sugar with them in cellophane pouches or glass jars. Two teenagers who were caught stealing sugar from a Missouri Pacific boxcar were severely chastised in the media, and sugar figured in at least one divorce, when the husband walked out with his wife's ration book. "Nothing but bitterness" remained, she said, "no sweets whatever."

In the months following Pearl Harbor the fear of sabotage by enemy aliens in the St. Louis area slowly abated. Operating under the U.S. Department of Justice, the St. Louis Enemy Alien Board was created and headed by Joseph A. McClain, dean of Washington University Law School. The board reviewed the cases of aliens held in custody. In mid-January it ruled that twenty-five of the twenty-six aliens who had been interned immediately after Pearl Harbor could be released from jail; fifteen were sent to army authorities and the rest were paroled or discharged. Only Tetsu Uyeda was left in custody, despite the fact that several influential St. Louisans spoke out in his behalf.

One letter-to-the-editor writer expressed the prevalent anti-Japanese sentiment when he suggested revamping an old slogan to "Don't fire until you see the slant of their eyes,"but another writer counseled tolerance. "Is 'V' for Victory or Vengeance?" he asked.

As the search for enemies within continued, the FBI began an investigation at St. John's Evangelical and Reformed Church in Chesterfield. Members of the congregation had charged their pastor, Rev. Fred H. Kalkbrenner, with sedition. Rev. Kalkbrenner had said, it was alleged, that the American government sanctioned brutality because it allowed the lynching of Negroes. (On January 25, 300 citizens of Sikeston, Missouri, had participated in a brutal lynching of a black man; authorities did not interfere.) Kalkbrenner also openly disliked the singing of the "Star-Spangled Banner" in church, and he collected money for conscientious objectors. Eventually Kalkbrenner was discharged from his church and left town.

Another suspect on the FBI's list was Otto Dingledein, founder and owner of St. Louis Silversmiths on Lindell. Not yet a naturalized citizen when war broke out, Dingledein was arrested and held in a downtown hotel incommunicado for two weeks. His frantic family could obtain no information on him until he was finally cleared of suspicion and released. Later, St. Louis Silversmiths was given a contract to make precision parts for bombers.

In late March the FBI made a sudden dinnertime raid on several homes in the area. They arrested six Germans and one Italian who were more obviously seditious. They had amassed an arsenal and a collection of Nazi paraphernalia, including rifles, shotguns, revolvers, swords, and bayonets. A telescope, short wave radio, and cameras were also seized, along with a Nazi Bund uniform, swastika armbands, and photographs of Hitler.

In July another German-born St. Louisan was arrested after he repeatedly told his co-workers at the Public Service Company that he

The Italian Anti-Fascist League, which met on the Hill, drew a large crowd of patriotic St. Louisans.

''wished all American soldiers could be lined up and shot down like dogs.'' The statement did not sit well with his fellow employees, who brought charges against him, claiming that his citizenship was invalid because he had not renounced his allegiance to the Third Reich.

But the vast majority of St. Louisans, whether native or foreign born, were loyal Americans. The Rumanian Beneficial and Cultural Society stated that it deeply regretted Rumania's declaration of war on the United States and voted to invest its surplus funds in defense bonds. Italian-Americans formed the Anti-Fascist League and supported all patriotic endeavors. In the fall of 1942, when tolerance was a bit easier, a Japanese-American girl from Los Angeles was admitted to Webster College without incident and with the approval of the student body.

In fact, most of the damage done in St. Louis war plants — and the FBI said there was ''a great deal of petty sabotage'' — was plain old American vandalism rather than an attempt to aid the enemy. At Curtiss-Wright a 22-year-old employee was arrested for using a machinist's ball peen hammer to break the bit of a drill. He said he did it in a ''spirit of meanness,'' because he was mad at the world, not to impede the war effort. Nonetheless his ''meanness'' nearly got him ten years in prison for sabotage.

One of the most patriotic gestures an American could make during the war was to buy defense bonds. The first week after Pearl Harbor, defense bond sales rose 121 percent. The Chamber's Thomas N. Dysart, chairman of the area's Defense Savings committee, organized a city-wide payroll deduction plan for buying bonds. Three hundred and fifty-eight firms adopted the plan right away and enrolled thousands of employees.

In May a star-studded Victory Caravan came through St. Louis to promote the bond drive. Over 12,000 St. Louisans crowded into the Municipal Auditorium to watch Jimmy Stewart, Groucho Marx, and dozens of other Hollywood celebrities make a pitch for buying bonds. They responded with $41,000.

Retail stores wholeheartedly joined the bond drive. Defense stamps were sold at Boyd's, Famous Barr, Stix Baer and Fuller, Sonnenfeld's, Garland's, Kline's, and Scruggs-Vandervoort-Barney. July was declared "Retailers for Victory Month." At noon on each working day all store business was halted for fifteen minutes and only bonds were sold. The first day brought in $225,000 in bonds and stamps. On July 17, "War Heroes Day," merchants distributed 250,000 postcards to people who bought stamps or bonds. The cards were to be sent to a favorite serviceman or woman.

The sale of bonds fluctuated with the interpretations of the war news. And in 1942 the war news was bleak indeed. In the Pacific, the U.S. Navy was struggling with its antiquated fleet and green personnel against the better equipped Japanese navy. The army, hoping to buy time, issued ancient rifles and ammunition to its troops while waiting for factories like U.S. Cartridge to catch up to the demand.

But despite the lack of defense materiel, the American forces had no lack of heroes. One of the first of the war was navy Lt. Edward ("Butch") O'Hare. O'Hare grew up in south St. Louis — his mother still lived on Bates Street — and attended Western Military Academy in Alton. While flying a combat mission in an F4F Wildcat in the Pacific in January, O'Hare was suddenly surrounded by eight Japanese bombers. In less than five minutes, he downed six of them and damaged a seventh. When he returned to St. Louis for a welcome-home parade in April after receiving the Medal of Honor, Mayor William Dee Becker said to him, "No mortal in all history has equaled what you have done . . . . Never, in aviation combat history, has such a mark been set before."

Capt. Eliott Vandeventer was another St. Louisan who became a hero. He won the Distinguished Flying Cross by sinking a Japanese transport and damaging three Japanese destroyers in the Philippines. He returned to St. Louis for a jubilant Fourth of July "war heroes parade."

Lt. Cmdr. Edward "Butch" O'Hare, St. Louis' first war hero, rated a mammoth parade on his first return home.

On April 18 a surprise bombing raid was made on four Japanese cities, including Tokyo. Leading the raid was former St. Louisan Col. James Doolittle. Although the attack did little damage — each plane carried only four bombs — seeing American forces take the offensive after four months of defeat after defeat gave Americans a much-needed dose of hope.

Phyllis Argall, a Canadian-born missionary and magazine correspondent in Japan at the time of Pearl Harbor, moved to St. Louis after being released from six months solitary confinement. She was the first Caucasian woman tried by the Japanese for espionage, and while several of her fellow correspondents were extensively tortured and even killed, she received relatively benign

treatment. She wrote of her experiences in *My Life With the Enemy.*
(Macmillan, 1944.)

Then, for hours on end, I would pace my cell. Three steps
and a turn, half a step and turn, three steps and turn again; I
paced until I wore smooth spots in the board floor.
Memorizing poetry helped there, too. Exercise was, I knew,
essential, and though theoretically we were allowed out for
seven minutes a day in a fenced cage in the yard, sometimes
days would pass and we would not get out. At first I paced
my cell through sheer inability to keep still. But soon poor
food and constant hemorrhages from which I suffered so
sapped my vitality that I had to drive myself to move. Then I
would set myself a stint of a certain number of lines to be
learned, and walk until I had learned them. If I sat down I
would, often as not, sink into a semicoma, and that I did not
dare to do. With the constant possibility of gendarmes coming to interrogate me, I was afraid to let my mind fog.

The nights were both the best and the worst. At night I
could close my eyes and dream, of people, of places where I
had been and would go, and, eventually, of food. But if I
dreamed, I sometimes also had nightmares, and woke
screaming. . . .

In spite of everything, however, I had one moment of excitement of which not even the guards could deprive me. It
was April 18, a Saturday. I was pacing my cell, at noon, as I
knew from the shadows thrown by the trees on the prison
walls, and I was thinking that in another three hours, four at
the most, I should get the ration of candies I had allowed
myself that day. But suddenly all thoughts of candies were
driven out of my head. I heard the rattling thunder of antiaircraft shells. I recognized the sound. . . . A moment later
the sirens blew. Then the wardens came around and double-
locked all doors. It could mean only one thing. American
planes were over Tokyo. I wanted to dance a jig, to get up
on the roof and wave, to cheer and yell. But all I could do
was sit in my cell, and hope.

The first flag-draped casket came home to St. Louis on June 11.
Eighteen-year-old Pvt. Otto J. Weiner, Jr., had been killed
''somewhere in the Pacific'' during heavy fighting. A requiem Mass
for all alumni of Catholic high schools who had been killed in action
was held at the St. Louis Cathedral the same month. The cathedral re-

A requiem mass was held at St. Louis Cathedral for the graduates of Christian Brothers College killed in 1942.

The caption for this Star-Times *editorial cartoon read, ''The real Spirit of St. Louis.''*

sounded with a triple salute of military rifles and ''Taps'' played by army buglers. Most young servicemen faced the possibility of their death with a show of bravado and counted on fate — or God — to get them through. Relatives of those killed took solace from the heroism of their soldier who had given his ''last full measure of devotion'' to the nation.

St. Louis suffered great losses in the Pacific during the 1942 campaign, at Bataan, on Corregidor, and in the Battle of the Coral Sea. St. Louisans were on the *Yorktown* and the *Lexington* when they went down. They were with Gen. Douglas MacArthur in his retreat from the Philippines and with Capt. Eddie Rickenbacker when he was shot down in the Pacific. Families at home could only wait, pray, hope, and pray some more. Each announcement of a lost sailor, soldier, pilot, or marine reminded St. Louisans of the crucial importance of producing war materiel.

Everyone was aware of the old rhyme that began ''For want of a nail'' and ended with ''a war was lost.'' Nails were made of metal — and so were machine guns, battleships, tanks, and hundreds of other necessities. But the supply of metal was woefully short of the demand. It was up to Americans to dig into their attics and cellars for scrap and make up the deficit.

In February 3,600 volunteers began a city-wide, door-to-door scrap drive for iron, steel, copper, brass, and lead. Matt C. Fogerty, mayor of University City and chairman of the county salvage committee, appealed to householders to take an inventory of their scrap. "Your old washing machine, worn-out garden tools or old water heating boiler might be the deciding shot to hurl at the Japs in the war," he said.

Immediately the Junk Peddlers Association objected. "This is taking the bread out of our mouths," said their spokesman. "It is competing with us and with our livelihood." Nonetheless, the drive continued and a depository was set up at the Hampton-Ruskin police station.

The use of metal, especially steel, was cut from the manufacture of hundreds of items. Consumers were instructed to use only one safety razor blade each week. They also were required to turn in an old toothpaste or shaving cream tube when buying a new one, because they were made of sheet lead. At that time Missourians were paying sales tax with mills. Each mill, which was about the size of a dime, was worth one-tenth of a cent and as stipulated by law was made of zinc. Eventually the Missouri legislature rescinded the law and millions of zinc mills were collected for the scrap drive. (Vinyl and cardboard ones replaced them.)

At the start of the drive in February, dealers in scrap were charged with both hoarding and profiteering — holding the scrap until they could get higher prices for it. Area steel companies, particularly Granite City Steel and General Steel Casting, claimed they would have to shut down unless dealers would cooperate. An investigation was launched. One St. Louis scrap dealer resented the implication. He stated that his firm processed about 5,000 tons of scrap per month and now had only 342 tons on hand, "an irreducible minimum."

"Only a few people out of an entire industry [are] guilty of practices not consistent with public interest,"he continued. "The majority are cooperating 100 percent."

Scrap collected in the St. Louis area went to the seven steel mills and forty-five foundries in the area. The mills produced steel for tanks, ships, and guns, and the foundries used scrap to turn out castings for machine tools and ship engines.

The scrap rubber campaign began officially on June 15. Fifteen hundred gas stations were designated collection points. People were encouraged to donate rubber, and most did, but stations were authorized to pay one cent for each pound. The national rubber demand in 1942 was for 874,000 tons, and only 459,000 tons were on hand. The projected demand for 1942 was for 1,047,000 tons. Although chemists were working day and night on the problem, no suitable synthetic rubber had yet been developed. Therefore, it was up to the American people to bring in their old tires, garden hoses, rubber boots, floor mats and even Kewpie dolls to meet the need. Mary and Michael Vesich,

Pots, pans, and pails were donated to the scrap drive.

Part of the growing mountain of scrap metal collected during 1942.

who operated a mom & pop grocery store on Manchester Road, offered to give free ice cream cones to any child who brought in a bit of rubber. When Mayor Becker refused to give up two miniature tires that served as ashtray holders, irate citizens impugned his patriotism: no scrap of rubber was too small to donate.

In August homemakers heard a plea for waste fat. Household grease could be converted into nitroglycerin. J. F. Padberg of the St. Louis Retail Meat Dealers' Association noted that St. Louis had about 280,000 households. If each household could save two ounces of fat every three weeks, the goal of 1,840,000 pounds could be easily reached. Mrs. T. M. (Louella) Sayman, civic leader and wife of an industrialist, chaired the Household Fats Conservation Commission and dozens

As this cartoon depicts, household fats were turned into nitroglycerin, which was used in the manufacture of ammunition.

of women's organizations spread the word. Grocery stores served as collection points.

With the slogan "Sock 'Em With Your Skillet!" homemakers were urged to join the "kitchen commandos" and contribute to the war effort by saving fat, recycling tin cans, and providing high- nutrition meals for their families without using more than their quota of meat, sugar, coffee, or any other goods that were in short supply. Laclede Gas Co. offered "Home Volunteer" badges to housewives to tell them how important their work was.

Homemakers enlisted in the campaign to salvage tin cans, beginning September 2. "Wash and squash" was the campaign's motto — each can was to be cleaned and flattened (with the lid inside). City garbage trucks picked up the cans the first Wednesday and Thursday of each month. Over half the households in St. Louis participated in the campaign and it was one of the most successful of the salvage drives during 1942.

As industry in the city boomed, wages rose and so did the pace of living. Freight movements in and out of the city increased by twenty-five percent and passenger movement by almost as much. Lambert Airport became the busiest airport in the United States, with nearly three times the number of takeoffs and landings as New York's LaGuardia Field. By the first anniversary of Pearl Harbor, as many as 125,000 newcomers had moved to St. Louis, most of them seeking jobs. Coincidentally, two new housing projects opened downtown, Carr Square Village and Clinton-Peabody Terrace. War workers were given first priority in the low-income housing. At the same time, on the north side, residents in the neighborhood of U. S. Cartridge were evicted to make room for the plant's expansion.

The influx of defense workers strained school facilities, particularly those in low-rent neighborhoods. Half-day sessions went into effect at Marshall and Lafayette schools. O'Fallon School, which had been closed during the depression, reopened. Twenty-seven additional teachers were assigned to the twenty schools in the growing district. Day-care centers for children too young to attend school opened throughout the city. Helen Wood, area YWCA director, advised out-of-town young women not to rush to St. Louis for jobs. "The entire pattern of living has been changed," she said, "and the character of the new section of the city completely altered." Fifty-four new taverns in Wellston alone had sprung up practically overnight. In Ferguson, as many as fifty families were living in trailers on one lot.

City police, concerned about the incidence of vice in the changing city, began a crack-down on prostitution. The L-shaped area along South Broadway, extending north to Franklin Avenue and west along Olive Street to Grand Boulevard, was dotted with cheap hotels and taverns which police called "breeding spots" for vice. Hotel bellboys often procured prostitutes for servicemen. (Unlike East St. Louis, St. Louis had few problems with street solicitation.) In June Dr. Joseph F. Bredeck, city health commissioner, claimed that because of vigorous prosecution, the number of houses of prostitution in the city had decreased from 165 at the start of the war to zero. There was a corresponding drop in the number of cases of venereal disease reported at Jefferson Barracks. But prostitution did not really disappear from St. Louis. It merely kept one step ahead of the vice squad.

In February, the month that year-round daylight savings time was initiated across America, an estimated 15,000 St. Louisans were working a night shift. By summertime, the number had tripled. To accommodate them, downtown stores began remaining open late on Mondays. The atmosphere was described as "like a mardi gras" downtown, as families strolled the streets and groups of young people in high spirits found outlets for their paychecks.

Sensing an audience, radio stations began broadcasting around the clock, movie theaters began presenting midnight shows, and bowling alleys opened for early morning leagues. The downtown YMCA offered volleyball, swimming and dancing from 11 P.M. to 4 A.M., and the Lafayette Baptist Church held a 2 A.M. service for war workers. Some of the late-night bowling teams in the ''Keep 'Em Rolling'' War League were the Curtiss-Wright Skyrockets, the McQuay-Norris Gunners, the McDonnell Aircraft Dodgers and the Emerson Electric Bombardiers.

Area USOs offered entertainment all hours of the day and night to men and women in the armed services. Staffed by volunteers, nine USOs in the city provided food, music and laughter. The largest (and noisiest) was located in the Municipal Auditorium and often attracted ''name'' entertainers. Rudy Vallee ''made the joint jump'' when he conducted the Coast Guard band through ''Mr. Five By Five'' there. Other USOs were located in the Y's. The USO at 6 S. Broadway was run by the Salvation Army, the one at 711 N. Grand by the St. Louis Catholic Archdiocese, at 724 Union by the YMHA-YWHA, and the one at 2909 Washington was for Negroes.

But the USOs couldn't house all the servicemen who came through St. Louis, so the army set up a ''recreational camp'' in Forest Park with enough tents for almost two thousand transient soldiers. St. Louisans were encouraged to ''take a soldier home for dinner.'' They also responded to the need for softening the hard edges of Jefferson Barracks. The Lions Club, PEO, Demolay Mothers, PTA, Garden Club, National Council of Jewish Women, and American Legion Auxiliary were among the organizations that provided easy chairs, records, pianos, curtains, plants, books, magazines and rugs for the day rooms at the barracks.

The Public Library initiated a ''Victory Books'' campaign for soldiers and collected new and used books for Jefferson Barracks and Fort Leonard Wood. Librarian Charles H. Compton reported that only two-thirds of the 45,000 volumes donated were usable. ''Soldiers are not particularly interested in *Mother Goose Complete, The Three Little Peppers and How They Grew,* or *Tasteful Decoration of the Guest Room,*'' he said. The library also promoted a ''Books and Bullets'' program. Almost a thousand books on engineering, aviation, and war production were circulated to give job seekers information in those fields.

Virtually every established organization in St. Louis had a program to further the war effort. Several new organizations were created just for that purpose. The American Women's Voluntary Service was established to provide services that other groups did not. Its ''button brigade'' mended clothes for servicemen. It also gathered photographs of foreign locales for the army and navy to glean information from, fingerprinted area children so they could be identified in case of a disaster, and collected old stockings to be used as bandages for burn

The dayroom at Jefferson Barracks, furnished largely by St. Louis service organizations, was a haven for recruits.

victims. Their "SOS" (Save Old Stockings) booth at the Fox Theater collected pounds of the valuable material.

A unique service for military men was offered by the St. Louis Bar Association. They gave free legal aid to servicemen and their wives and were able to stop at least one foreclosure on a home. Attorney George M. Hagee commented on the case, "You can't make $50 a month payments on $21 a month [the average GI's pay]." The Missouri attorney general later ruled that the property of a serviceman could not be repossessed for the duration.

The most active organization in support of servicemen during the war was the American Red Cross, "the greatest mother of them all." Sidney Maestre, St. Louis banker and tireless fund-raiser for the Red Cross, noted the "tremendous tasks for our armed forces on every front. No less tremendous is the task of the Red Cross as it serves side by side with our troops everywhere." The Red Cross trained hundreds of nurse's aides in St. Louis and gave thousands of first aid certificates. (At least two accident victims in 1942 owed their lives to graduates of

Red Cross first aid courses who were in the right place at the right time.) It was able to cut through military red tape and to enable family members to communicate with each other when all other avenues seemed closed. And it secured thousands of units of blood for the wounded. The day after the St. Louis Cardinals won the World Series by beating the New York Yankees in five games, the entire team went to the Red Cross headquarters, rolled up their sleeves and donated blood.

In 1942 St. Louis was one of the most segregated cities in the nation. In 1916 its voters had passed an ordinance which enforced residential segregation by making it illegal for persons of one race to move to a block where seventy-five percent of the residents were of another race. Schools, hotels, movie theaters, barber shops, and restaurants were segregated. Blacks who worked downtown had to bring lunch with them if they wanted to eat at midday, for no restaurant, cafe, or cafeteria in the area would serve them.

In Sikeston, Missouri, on January 25, 1942, a black man was accused of accosting a white woman. As he tried to flee he was shot three times by the sheriff and was carried unconscious but still alive to the local jail. A crowd of about 300 whites gathered outside the jail, demanding that "something be done." Something was. A group of men broke into the jail, dragged the wounded man out and tied him to the rear of a car. After dragging him to a specified location, they doused him with gasoline and set him afire.

Lynching at that time was not legal, but local officials in southern states often looked resolutely in the opposite direction when it happened. An outraged editorial in the *New York Times,* a formal protest from the ACLU, and a shaking of heads among church people was usually the extent of white reaction. But this time the reaction was stronger. On February 2 six thousand St. Louisans met at the Negro YMCA on Pine Street to protest the Sikeston lynching. The meeting was led by local NAACP president Sidney R. Redmond and Mayor Becker.

Blacks met often during 1942 to protest their exclusion from American society. Theodore McNeal, who became Missouri's first black state senator, was closely aligned with A. Philip Randolph's "March on Washington" campaign during 1942. The march was designed to tell President Roosevelt, Congress and the American people that black workers wielded a power that must be reckoned with. Blacks wanted equal opportunity in the military, in jobs, and in housing. The St. Louis Urban League asked that the black man "be allowed to use all his skills, all his talents and all his courage in fighting in the army and navy, side by side with his white brothers."

WAKE UP NEGROES!

FIGHT FOR LIFE!

WE DIE FOR FREEDOM **BUT** **WE LIVE BY BREAD!!**

WITHOUT JOBS - WHAT GOOD IS FREEDOM?

25,000 NEGROES TO STORM THE AUDITORIUM, 14th & MARKET STS.

(ADMISSION FREE)

FRI. NITE, AUG. 14 - 7 P. M.

DEMANDING JOBS AND PROTESTING

1. Jim-Crow St. Louis Labor Unions and War Plants.
2. Lynching at Sikeston and Texarkana.
3. Mobbing and Shooting Our Boys in Uncle Sam's Uniform.
4. Violation of Pres. Roosevelt's Order No. 8802.
5. Jim-Crow Policy of the Navy, Army and U. S. Marines.
6. Insult of the Red Cross in Segregating Negro Blood.

JOIN THE MARCH--SWELL THE NUMBERS

Fight For The Right To Live - Work and Be Free

MARCH ON WASHINGTON COMMITTEE

Headquarters: 412 Finance Bldg. - 11 N. Jefferson - FR. 0033

"Winning Democracy for the Negro Is Winning the War for Democracy"

The war years saw the beginning of the modern civil rights movement. This poster urges blacks to get involved in the struggle.

Civil rights marchers asked for jobs in 1942.

The first St. Louis blacks were sworn into the navy on June 1. On April 7 the navy, marines, and coast guard had agreed to allow blacks to serve in capacities other than messmen, but refused to allow them a commission. All branches of the service remained segregated until President Harry S. Truman's executive order integrated them in the closing days of the war.

A survey in the fall of 1942 showed that about 8,000 black men and women had found employment in war industries, but there were about five blacks jobless for each one hired. The Chamber of Commerce circulated a letter urging area manufacturers to hire blacks, as well as women, older workers and the handicapped because "discrimination limits production." Discrimination also created an artificial labor shortage which brought in more newcomers to St. Louis, straining the city's resources still further.

At that time only 800 blacks were working at U.S. Cartridge, the city's largest employer, and most of them were in unskilled jobs. So that plant was the target of the first demonstration here against discrimination in employment. Emerson Electric, Curtiss-Wright, and Wagner Electric began training blacks (including women) for skilled jobs in the summer of 1942. Curtiss-Wright and Atlas Powder instituted all-Negro

Western Historical Manuscript Collection, Thomas Jefferson Library, UMSL

Western Historical Manuscript Collection, Thomas Jefferson Library, UMSL

Red Cross POW packages were a most welcome reminder of home.

Red Cross volunteers put in thousands of hours and freed medical professionals for service in the military.

production units. Scullin Steel employed more blacks in skilled jobs than any other employer in 1942; over half of its work force of 2,000 was black.

Many women, especially young women, were finding the war the most liberating adventure of their lives. In May the army established the WAACs and a few months later the navy created the WAVEs as auxiliaries. St. Louis women were eager to join both. For those who stayed at home, plenty of work was available. White women made up about one-third of the work force at U. S. Cartridge Co. and looked "very smart in brown fatigue caps, brown slacks and blouses." Their outfits (which they were required to buy) cost $1.98 each. The starting pay for women in most of the defense industries was fifty-one cents an hour, about half that for men, and the most they could hope for was fifty-nine cents an hour. About midway through 1942 the minimum age for female employees was lowered from eighteen to sixteen.

In July each major defense plant nominated a favorite woman worker for the title of "Miss Victory of 1942." Each of the contestants interviewed said she was delighted to be working in a factory. All the women were former cigarette girls, waitresses, and sales clerks who had been making about half their present wages. Darline Long of McQuay-Norris was selected as Miss Victory. She later left her post there to join the armed forces.

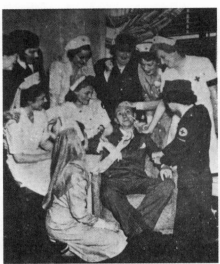

In a skit presented at the Chase Hotel, Red Cross volunteers offer aid to Wallace Smith, a "victim." From left, front row: Mrs. Tom Pettus, Mrs. M. B. Clark, Mrs. Harry Wuertenbaecher. Back row: Mrs. S. I. Sievers, Mrs. John A. Scudder, Mrs. Lee Neidringhaus, and Mrs. Robert E. Mudkins. Mrs. Robert Sherman kneels in front.

Women also found opportunities to use their talents in non- paid Red Cross, USO, and civil defense work. The first woman air raid warden, like the first woman welder or radio operator or taxi driver, was a novelty, but soon the novelty wore off and women in all work capacities were accepted.

As the cost of living began to skyrocket soon after the declaration of war, the fear of runaway inflation led to the creation of the national Office of Price Administration (OPA). Beginning May 18, all stores in the country were required to post ceiling prices of commodities. Many prices were cut back to November 1941 levels.

St. Louis merchants generally saw price controls as a "good thing." Victor Oehlert, manager of Schmiemeier Pharmacy at Gravois and Jefferson said, "What is good for the public is good for the merchants. There has been a lot of groaning about high prices, and maybe the price ceilings will make everyone feel better." However many of the area's 12,000 retail stores failed to comply with the directives and consumer complaints were often lost in the shuffle of paperwork.

In July Grover C. Vandover was named rent arbitrator for St. Louis. He was given wide discretionary powers to control rent costs in the city and county of St. Louis and in four surrounding counties. After his office was deluged with complaints about rising rents, he stressed the fact that rent ceilings were not intended to ensure fair rents, only stable rents.

Small businesses, as well as small retail outlets, found price controls coupled with material and manpower shortages a serious hardship. At least 300 small businesses in Missouri were in trouble in 1942. Leo Lau told a senate investigating committee holding hearings in St. Louis in November that the navy had taken over his 4,000-barrel-a-day oil refinery in April and then abandoned it without compensating him. "Now we have no money, the navy has our plant, it won't pay us and no one will tell us what to do," he lamented.

Shortages of cloth meant a radical revision of the fashion industry, which the St. Louis garment district took in stride. The specifications released in April forbade cuffs for pants and sleeves, wool trim, hoods, shawls, capes, scarfs, overskirts, patch pockets, flaps, and belts. The length of skirts and coats was prescribed. Jean Lawson, a secretary with the Maternal Welfare Association, voiced the opinion of the new style echoed by many St. Louis women. "We'll be better off without the frills," she said.

When St. Louis designers unveiled their "L-85" fashions in July (the number refers to the number of the directive restricting yardage), they met with applause. But almost all St. Louis clothing manufacturers had replaced *Vogue* with *Stars and Stripes* and were working around the clock to turn out uniforms, battle jackets, military caps, parachutes, field tents, and the other accoutrements of war.

Labor unrest in St. Louis began when the first glow of patriotism faded, only months after the declaration of war. By late spring unauthorized wildcat strikes were called almost daily. Both the AFL and the CIO claimed full support for the war effort — and indeed gave generously to the Red Cross, bought bonds, and collected scrap — yet some of their members continually stymied local defense production and frustrated businessmen trying to meet deadlines. Business itself was under fire for making excess profits because of the war. A ninety-nine percent tax on profits was enacted and salaries for executives in war industries were frozen at $25,000. Emerson Electric and its president, Stuart Symington, were closely scrutinized by a Congressional investigating committee for signs of profiteering. Both came through with not only a clean bill of health, but a commendation for good management.

In September President Roosevelt announced glumly that war production hadn't been "half enough" and urged workers to increase their efforts. The War Production Board gave high recognition to workers who came up with ideas that would make assembly lines more efficient. Burnell E. Stewart, an assembly methods engineer at Curtiss-Wright, was one of seventeen war plant workers in the United States who was commended in September for an idea. He suggested using wood fiber punching jigs instead of steel jigs, which cut operating time by one half.

As fall began, St. Louis' children brought enthusiasm and energy to the war effort. All year they had saved nickels and dimes to buy defense stamps, and prepared Red Cross "buddy kits" for soldiers overseas. Boy Scouts and Girl Scouts volunteered to help householders tend their victory gardens, and high school students in machine shop made hundreds of precise scale model airplanes for the armed forces.

Fourteen-year old Fred Starr threw all of his considerable energy into the war effort. Every day after school he worked as a messenger for the Office of Civil Defense, walking five to ten miles delivering notices and press releases. When he got home he made beanbag boards and ashtrays out of tin cans for the USO and writing tables and stretchers for the Red Cross. On Saturdays he checked coats at a USO or served soft drinks in the canteen. Word about his dedication got out. He was chosen Quiz Kid "Boy of the Month" and his story was told on that national radio program.

The scrap drive was faltering until the Fanchon-Marco theater chain decided to involve the children of the city. In mid-August they offered a free pinto pony to the child who brought the most rubber salvage and another to the one who brought the most metal salvage to a special matinee at three of its theaters — the Fox, the Missouri and the St. Louis — on September 5. The response was so great that twenty-nine theaters were added to the list and many other prizes were offered, including Gene Autry cowboy suits and baseballs autographed by the St. Louis Browns. Every child who collected at least one pound of rubber or five pounds of metal got a a free ticket to the show.

Noting the enthusiasm generated by the drive, the school districts enlisted their 150,000 elementary school children in a "mammoth roundup of scrap metal" in late September. It turned out to be a drive that "will never be forgotten," said St. Louis school superintendent Philip J. Hickey. Using wagons, homemade two-wheel trailers, ponies, and even a taxi, the kids scoured the city, fearlessly knocking on doors and looking in long-abandoned garages and basements.

Their booty included cavalry swords of the Civil War, helmets from World War I, an 1887 Morris typewriter found in a storeroom of an office building, a loving cup award from an 1897 sharpshooting contest, an old slot machine still full of nickels, a 1925 automobile and a metal urn filled with ashes. One father came home from work to find the furnace he had painstakingly taken apart to clean was missing. (He recovered all the parts.)

Competition among the schools in the one-month drive was fierce and the lead changed hands daily. Riverview Gardens gave its students a day off to search for scrap and the school district even provided twelve trucks for hauling. Divoll School suffered a serious setback when 20,000 pounds of its best scrap was stolen.

Hyatt School, a ten-student, one-room school on Shackleford Road near Florissant collected the most scrap in the area, with a staggering

1,000 pounds per student. Their prize was the chance to send a student to the christening of a Liberty ship. Twelve-year old Leroy Loesing was chosen to represent Hyatt. In the city contest another small school, Bethany Lutheran, took first place. Parochial schools in the city outdid public schools by a wide margin. Altogether the schools collected a total of 6,300 tons.

The school scrap drive gave heart to the city scrap drive. The Congress of Industrial Organizations enlisted 60,000 of its workers to find bits of scrap that other scavengers had missed. University City named Columbus Day as the day to uncover enough scrap to make 37,000 hand grenades. Mayor Fogerty himself dismantled a jail cell door for the drive. The Kirkwood scrap drive brought in 200 tons, and East St. Louis collected 500 tons in one day.

St. Louis' scrap party was held October 23. The streets around city hall were blocked off. The Jefferson Barracks band played martial music while Bierman Iron & Metal Company contributed its old roof. The gates from Union Station went into the heap; so did the fences from around Lafayette Park and City Hospital and about 50,000 pounds of ancient traffic signals. Four World War I tanks from Jefferson Barracks were donated. And the Washington University Bears gave up the locomotive wheel rim that had long been their symbol of victory — it was struck each time the Bears scored a touchdown.

Will Doctor, a Union Market wholesale meat dealer, gave the bumpers from nine automobile and trucks. He had replaced the chrome bumpers with ones made from oak. The city also put out a call for keys — it hoped to collect seven million of them. Nearly one million were collected the first week in October. Area beauty and barber shops donated old chairs, barber poles and other equipment to the scrap drive. In New York, former St. Louisan Helen Traubel threw Brunhilde's spear and shield on the scrap pile.

Civil Defense was not forgotten in the drive to find scrap. Ferguson was the first community in the state of Missouri to stage an air raid drill in April 1942. Nine "enemy planes" from Sylvan Beach Airport scored twenty-seven "hits" before they were driven off.

The city of St. Louis finally had its air raid warning system operational in early May. All available steam whistles and sirens sounded a warning — on five seconds and off three seconds — for two minutes on May 12. The results were disappointing. There were innumerable "dead spots" where nothing was heard at all, and everyone agreed that the noise wasn't loud enough to wake anyone up.

The second air raid test was held on November 13 and 4,500 air raid wardens participated. This time seventy factory whistles, fifty-two fixed sirens, forty police car sirens and innumerable railroad whistles sounded for two cacophonous minutes and no one complained that they couldn't hear anything. The city's dogs added their bit by joining in with patriotic howls.

St. Louis dogs also enlisted in the Dogs for Defense canine corps and served their country in stations as far away as the Solomon Islands. Cats too did their part. A tomcat walked into the St. Louis Ordnance district office on Lindell in November and took charge of a situation that was bordering on chaos. Odds were two to one that when a file drawer was opened, a mouse would jump out, causing considerable panic among personnel. With "supreme self-assurance,"the cat — now named Ammunition Pete — set to work and restored serenity to the office. As a reward, Pete was given an ID badge and free access to all departments and files. He also got his own box.

Two months of planning went into a nine-state blackout held on December 14. The area involved encompassed 712,000 square miles and 15,000,000 people. The blackout began at 9:58 P.M. and lasted twenty minutes. It was, said Colonel McBride, "nearly perfect." Only a few forgetful householders left their lights on or neglected to use blackout curtains. Reporters viewing the event from on top the Civil Courts building described the eerie feeling that took hold of them as they watched the city darken. The deep darkness and the intense quiet seemed to transform the city into a never-never land.

During the blackout a baby boy was born without incident at Missouri Baptist Hospital. Coincidentally, a surprise mock attack was staged at Jefferson Barracks, complete with several kinds of gas. But the defenders were well drilled and responded quickly enough to fight the attackers off.

The night after the blackout, a real emergency occurred. A B-24 Liberator apparently was unable to gain the necessary altitude after taking off from Lambert Airport and crashed three miles north of the field at Dunn Road and Utz Lane in Florissant. As it descended, it sheared away part of the barn on the Orval Brixey farm and set on fire the home of Reginald Crouse. Mrs. Crouse and her three-month-old baby ran from the house as it burst into flames. The plane broke in half. Seven men in the fuselage died as it exploded; two men in the tail — which landed 500 feet from the flaming wreck — walked away.

As early as April, a gasoline shortage was evident on the East Coast. Despite assurances that there would be no need for gas rationing in the Midwest, the shortage slowly spread across the country. In August Secretary of the Interior Harold L. Ickes prohibited the transport of gasoline to Missouri and ten other states because it was needed so desperately in the East. St. Louis had enough reserves and nearby refineries to last a while, but unless supplies could be replenished, gas rationing was inevitable.

The first week in November, motorists were instructed that they

Buses line up at U.S. Cartridge to take shift workers home. Without public transportation the city would have been immobilized by gasoline and tire rationing.

must apply for A, B, or C ration books. Most received A books, which entitled them to four gallons of gasoline per week, allowing them to travel about 240 miles per month. Those with extraordinary transportation needs got B or C books. (St. Louis' three Congressmen — John J. Cochran, Walter C. Ploeser and John B. Sullivan — and Missouri Senator Harry S. Truman each took advantage of the governmental X card, which gave them unlimited gas.)

Gas rationing officially began on December 1. Traffic dropped by as much as fifty percent as St. Louisans turned to car pooling and public transportation. County residents began moving to the city. About ten percent of the area's gas stations closed. The decrease in traffic was probably a good thing, since all street repairs had been halted because of the scarcity of cement. The night before the order went into effect, gas stations were swamped with cars wanting one last fill-up.

At the same time that gasoline rationing went into effect, fuel oil rationing also began. City high school math students were enlisted to compute the complicated formulas for the 35,000 fuel oil users in the area. Each of the ten high schools received 3,500 cases and each computation was said to take thirty minutes. The amount to be allocated for the winter of 1942-43 was based on the amount of square footage that had been heated in the past, the special requirements of the user and a few other factors.

Fuel oil rationing turned out to be a severe hardship. Everyone was suposed to be given one-third to one-half of the previous year's amount, but often even that was unavailable. Otis E. Welch, for instance, used 800 gallons in the winter of 1941-42 to heat his three-room flat. He was given 380 gallons for 1942-43, and he had three small children to care for, including a four-month-old baby. The elderly also suffered from both the cold and the frustration of trying to fight a bureaucracy.

Customers complained that the forms that were needed in order to receive an allocation of fuel oil were a "crossword puzzle maze" and beyond the ability of the average person to understand. Long lines formed at the offices of the St. Louis rationing board. It sometimes took four hours simply to reach the information desk, and then the long-suffering applicant often heard that the form he was clutching was the wrong one. Consumers were told to convert to coal, whether or not that was possible. "It's an outrage," was the most common comment. Electric heaters sold out in all area stores.

City cultural institutions responded to the war in both subtle and obvious ways. The City Art Museum placed buckets of sand in each of its galleries in readiness for incendiary bombs and held a special exhibit called "Art and War." Museums on the East Coast asked St. Louis to house some of their precious exhibits for the duration, and for a while officials considered storing all art in a cave outside the city. The Missouri Botanical Garden held a Victory Harvest Show in October, which became an annual event for the duration. Produce from victory gardens was exhibited along with military displays; the highlight of the show was a special induction of navy recruits.

The cast and crew of *Showboat,* a Muni Opera presentation, donated an entire performance to the Army-Navy Relief Fund, and the show was transmitted via shortwave radio to troops stationed all over the world. A long-time favorite excursion boat, *The City of St. Louis,* built in 1907, enlisted in the Coast Guard as a dredge. The Warwick, Congress, and Stevens hotels were converted into barracks.

Washington University and Saint Louis University offered tuition-free defense schools to potential war workers, which taught them the elements of engineering. The two universities also telescoped their medical programs into three years in order to produce more doctors for the military. At least ten percent of St. Louis' doctors were drafted; about seventy-five percent of recent medical school graduates went into the military.

The Veiled Prophet announced early in the war that his parade and ball would be canceled for the duration. However, the parade in very different form was held as scheduled in October. Shattering tradition,

The Order of the Eastern Star bought several ambulances for the Hospital Corps at Jefferson Barracks.

the Prophet was escorted by five women who symbolized civilian efforts to keep the home front strong. Only nine floats participated in the parade and they all pertained to the war effort. The parade kicked off the War Chest drive, which temporarily replaced the Community Chest. Rather than hosting a ball, the Prophet invited the city to an elaborate program at the Municipal Auditorium emceed by movie favorite Conrad Nagel.

Ironically, despite the daily emphasis on the virtues of democracy, the election of November 1942 saw one of the lowest voter turnouts in history. Only twenty-three percent of the registered voters in the St. Louis area voted. And in spite of vigorous campaigning by opponents, the so-called "isolationist" Congressmen — those who had wanted the United States to stay out of war — were returned, representative Walter C. Ploeser among them.

On November 8 the Allies invaded North Africa and faced the Afrika Korps of Nazi General Erwin Rommel. After six months of bloody battling, Rommel abandoned the continent and gave the Allies their first clear-cut success. The African campaign was one of endurance in the tough climate and rugged terrain. The lack of roads across the desert severely hindered the advance of the Allies, whose tanks were no match for the German Panzers. Gruendler Crusher of St. Louis provided some of the equipment that was used to build roads in North Africa.

As the second Christmas of the war approached, shortages cut into the buying mood. Coffee was almost unobtainable (it was later rationed), milk, cheese, and bacon were scarce, diapers were difficult to find, and alarm clocks all but impossible. In response to the later shortage an enterprising woman in University City began a telephone wake-

The Community Chest was renamed the War Chest during the duration, but kept the familiar red feather.

up service to compensate for the scarcity of alarm clocks. Her business became very successful.

Many gift items had vanished from stores — small electrical appliances, radios, imported hams, typewriters, silk ties, nylon hose, pure woolen and linen goods, and gin. Only wooden, plastic, or gold jewelry was available, and cotton or rayon neckties replaced silk ones. Fishermen's and hunter's boots were gone and golf equipment was scarce. Many Christmas toys were made of wood or pasteboard. There were very few erector sets, coasters, wagons, tricycles, electric trains or rubber dolls. "Victory" doll buggies and "battle wagons" were made of wood. Tin soldiers gave way to cardboard ones. Stores reported that games were big sellers, especially target games, an airplane spotter game and a blackout game. General MacArthur dolls and war plant worker dolls (in slacks and hairnet, rather than in bouffant skirts and permanent waves) were popular.

A unique gift for servicemen and women was offered by Famous-Barr. Relatives and friends could make a recording at the canteen because "your hero wants to hear your voice." The six-inch record plus mailing envelope sold for twenty-five cents.

Almost everyone's list for Santa Claus in 1942 carried one word: peace. Congregation Brith Sholom was especially mindful of the need for peace as it designated a solemn Day of Mourning for the Jews killed by Hitler.

Martha Cunliff, assistant editor of the *Curtiss-Wrighter,* won first prize in the *Charm Magazine* contest for the best letter to Santa. She expressed for for many young women the frustrations of the time. She wrote,

DEAR SANTA,

A lot of serious thinking went into this letter before I finally decided what I wanted this Christmas.

At first I thought I'd ask for victory and peace — but those are things that must be won and are not to be had merely for the wishing.

Then I knew what I wanted, not only for myself, but for thousands of girls like me. Dear Santa, could you possibly — please — give me a whole 24 hours to spend just as I like? Just 24 hours away from the pounding roar of a rivet gun, away from the agonzied death shriek of metal as it goes under the cutter. For a whole year now, ever since December 7, we victory workers have been working six, sometimes seven, days a week, and a whole day to ourselves would be heaven!

Would you like to know how I'd spend it? First I'd sleep late, until 9 or so. Then after breakfast, I'd go to town and shop leisurely for that devastating hat I want . . . and need so badly. To lunch, then, with another girl at a big hotel, where we would see a lot of old friends we haven't seen for months.

Next a visit to the Art Museum to renew an old friendship with a certain pair of Ming dogs, as well as the rest of their Chinese collection. A date for cocktails and dancing, then, with Jim, and home to dress before going to dinner with Bill.

We'd take our time over dinner and dance until the musicians yawned openly and laid away their instruments. There'd be a moon on the way home, and Bill would whisper all the things I want to hear him say. And when he kissed me good night, I'd know that all my tomorrows would be taken care of.

That's my wish for Christmas, St. Nick — just one whole day, 24 hours out of eternity, to live just like that.

Martha F. Cunliff

P.S. Of course, you know it can't really happen, because — Jim was killed on Bataan, and Bill — Bill's "somewhere in the Pacific," with no word from him in months. But there are hundreds of thousands of girls, Santa, who have the same wish, I know, so try to arrange it for them, won't you please? Merry Christmas!

Christmas Day was an ordinary working day for defense workers, just as Thanksgiving had been and just as New Year's Day would be.

Gen. Douglas MacArthur, struggling for control of New Guinea, sent a special Christmas message to the men and women at Monsanto Chemical Company thanking them for the production of "the sinews of war that make our victory possible."

After a year at war, St. Louisans knew there were more years of work ahead of them and they buckled down for the long haul. The coming of the new year brought the hope that things would get better, but the mood was not overly optimistic. The battle of the Coral Sea in May had been inconclusive; the fight for Guadalcanal was still raging; no good news had come from North Africa. Singapore, Mandalay, Rangoon, Bataan, Corregidor, Tobruk, and Sevastopol had fallen. Hitler occupied all of France and most of western Europe. The Russians were surrounded at Stalingrad. The June 4 battle of Midway would later be recognized as a turning point in the Pacific war, but Americans did not know that in December. Nonetheless, the nation had survived a grueling year — its people were tougher than anyone had imagined. And on the East Coast, precisely at midnight on December 31, the torch of the Statue of Liberty flashed its defiant message to the Axis powers: ... —, international Morse code for the letter "V," which to the Allies meant only one thing — victory.

THE SECOND YEAR — 1943
ENDURANCE

THE YEAR 1943 BEGAN with the realization that we were deep into a "long war, a bloody war, a costly war," as one general declared. Humphrey Bogart had "a date with fate" in Casablanca. So did Franklin Roosevelt and British Prime Minister Winston Churchill. In a secret meeting there in January the Allies decided to accept only an unconditional surrender from the Axis. No halfway measures would do. It was time, said Roosevelt and Churchill, for "more intense prosecution of the war by land, sea and air." It was time for attack.

Early in the year a trickle of good news came from the two fronts. Steadily and systematically, U.S. Marines were clearing Guadalcanal in the Solomon Islands of Japanese. The Russian army had survived the seige of Stalingrad and was beginning to push the Nazis out of the Soviet Union. And American radar combined with British U-boat hunters were turning the tide in the battle of the Atlantic.

In St. Louis the year was less than one week old when five inspectors — all former employees — brought charges against U.S. Cartridge in St. Louis for allowing defective shells to pass inspection. Shells with cracked heads not only would not fire, they also jammed machine guns, effectively disarming the troops. The FBI and the army ordnance division had been in the process of examining conditions at the plant when the story broke. After the January 4 headlines in the *Star Times,* which claimed "Unfit Shells Pass Plant Inspection," the plant was "deluged" with investigators from various government agencies. Sen. Harry S. Truman promised to bring his investigative commission to the city if necessary. (The Truman Commission was building a reputation as the watchdog of the defense industry.)

Those bringing charges signed affidavits that they had been in-

Workers at the St. Louis ordnance plant turned out millions of cartridges for the armed forces.

structed to place inferior and obviously defective cartridges at the bottom of cartons before U.S. Army inspectors arrived. Other employees claimed that powder was loaded into cases still wet after being washed and supposedly dried, or into cases containing grease or oil from production machines. U.S. Cartridge replied in full-page newspaper ads that the implications of the charges were unfair. Each cartridge leaving the plant was subject to dozens of inspections by ''eagle-eyed'' and totally honest inspectors, it said. Everyone wanted to win the war and U.S. Cartridge was doing its utmost to help.

When the army investigation fizzled out and officials stated that inspection at the St. Louis plant was no worse than at any other ammunition plant, a grand jury was called. Their inquiry into the charges dragged on all year. The results were announced on December 21, when the United States government, through district attorney Harry C. Blanton, formally charged ten employees of U.S. Cartridge with faulty inspection. Three counts of the wartime sabotage act were invoked: causing defective ammunition to be manufactured, conspiracy to defraud the government, and submission of false claims to the government. Two thousand dollars in damages was sought for each alleged violation from both the contractor (U.S. Cartridge) and the army ordnance department.

Those arrested were not top-level executives, but on-line inspectors, who said they resented being "scapegoats" and "fall guys" for U.S. Cartridge. One of those arrested said that he often rejected shells as defective, but they came back repeatedly until he finally let them pass. "It was agony every hour I worked there," he said.

In April 1944 five of the indicted employees were acquitted. Three of the others admitted that they had passed defective cartridges "on orders of their superiors." Charges against them were not pressed. A civil suit was continued until 1953, when the District Court and the Court of Appeals ruled that that U.S. Cartridge had "made every reasonable effort to maintain a satisfactory inspection system and could not be held liable for occasional unauthorized acts of a few employees."

Rumors had been circulating for a long time that the great ferris wheel from the 1904 World's Fair had been buried in Forest Park near Skinker Boulevard. In January search teams with metal detectors began looking for it — it would be a valuable contribution to the scrap metal drive.

At the end of January, a three-foot long bolt and section of an angle beam were uncovered, and the search intensified for the the seventy-ton axle, spurred on by the memories of a World's Fair maintenance man. The ninth fairway of the golf course seemed a good location, but it was necessary to break through a concrete slab in order to reach the most likely spot. The destruction to the park that followed angered the mayor and several vocal citizens who called for an end to the search. If indeed the ferris wheel and its parts were still buried in the park, they ought to rest in peace. As compensation for the lost ferris wheel, which was never found, the mayor ordered the ornamental cannons from City Hall cut up for scrap. The city also gave 200 unused iron trolley poles and the fence around Lyon Park. At the Old Federal Building, ancient air compressors were broken up and carted out to the scrap pile.

"We will win when our fat heads and fat bodies have been trained down to fighting trim," Dr. Frank Sullivan, professor of English at Saint Louis University and civil defense vice chairman, said in 1942. In 1943 fat bodies, at least, were definitely on their way out.

With somewhat of a shock, Americans woke up early in the year to learn that there wasn't enough food to go around. The government's solution was food rationing, using a system of points. Simply put, point rationing meant that the scarcest foods — sirloin steak, for instance — were assigned the greatest number of points and the least popular foods, like canned sauerkraut, got the least number. Practically all processed food, in cans, jars, and bottles, dried or frozen, was rationed and its consumption cut in half. Baby food was not rationed and the sale of strained fruits and vegetables soared as ingenious homemakers experimented with new recipes.

When first announced, the point rationing system seemed so complicated that civil defense volunteers were enlisted to explain the procedure. The system required shoppers to plan a full month's menu in advance, which few people had the time or inclination to do. The St. Louis school system took on the task of organizing a house-to-house campaign in January to explain point rationing as part of its adult education program. A total of 18,000 volunteers fanned out to visit 250,663 dwelling places. "It [the educational campaign] is the largest thing of its kind ever done here — revolutionary," said school superintendent Philip J. Hickey.

OCD official Charles H. Ellaby uses a torch to cut up a German tank tread.

As volunteers explained, each family was allowed to have five cans of food on hand when point rationing began. If any more were claimed, coupons for them had to be removed from the book. Each person, regardless of age, was allowed 48 points per month. Nine different point values were assigned to food. Rationing covered all edible meats as well as processed food.

An eleventh hour jam at the rationing office tied up traffic for hours. Two thousand people were turned away because they lacked the first rationing book (for sugar), which had been issued in May 1942. The government required proof of possession of the #1 book before the new, #2(general) one could be issued.

On the fifth floor of Stix Baer and Fuller department store, a model grocery was set up where instructors attempted to teach seasoned housewives how to shop for food. A suggested wartime menu offered pig heart, potato soup, parsnips, and soybean crackers. Cereals, which were abundant, appeared in a dozen different guises. In contrast to the struggle that civilians were experiencing, soldiers at Jefferson Barracks and Scott Field were reported to be dining on roast beef and steak.

Most homemakers were stoical about the changes. Mrs. Lewis Parker, who registered for a rationing book at Madison School, said, "If the boys in the front lines can do their part, I think the least we can do is accept this without complaining."

Retail grocers tried to sort out the confusing regulations in order to explain them to consumers. A typical grocery ad claimed, "Point for point we'll make your dollar go farther." The amount of food allowed

St. Louisans were backed up for blocks along Olive Street, awaiting issuance of ration books at the Eugene Field School.

to restaurants was cut in half, and restaurants which closed one day a week to save ration points had their allotments cut even further. A check of stores on March 1 showed that few homemakers had made plans to spread points over the entire month in any systematic way.

Coffee substitutes, which were made primarily with cereal grains, did not require a coupon, but few people drank them with pleasure. The standard coffee ration was one pound for each person fourteen years of age or older per six-week period.

The meat shortage hit Americans hard. At the first of the year, the demand for beef equaled twice the supply. One meat manager in St. Louis reported getting five dressed cattle per week where he used to get twelve. By March 1 the meat shortage was acute. Stores sold out of everything except hamburger, sausage, and lunch meats. "People who used to look down their noses at chuck roast are tickled to death to get it nowadays," one butcher said.

One solution to the meat shortage was to use exotic meats. When muskrat stew was served to fourteen prominent St. Louisans at the Mark Twain Hotel, Thomas N. Dysart reported, "muskrat is delish!" It was labeled "Marsh Rabbit ala Louisiana," soaked in vinegar for thirty minutes and seasoned with salt, pepper, celery, garlic, bay leaves, and sugar. Then onions and mushrooms were added and the dish was simmered for another thirty minutes. Result: rave reviews. Kuhs Deep Freeze Company distributed five thousand pounds of muskrat meat here at thirty cents per pound.

Empty meat counters and forlorn butchers became a familiar sight at Will Doctor's Meat Market in Union Market.

Four tons of shark were shipped in from Seattle. Shortages of halibut, salmon, and cod made shark seem attractive, although it was never popular here. Horse meat, too, was offered in St. Louis. Some 60,000 pounds sold for twenty-five to thirty cents per pound. A horse meat dinner (called "filly of cheval" was eaten "with gusto" at the Missouri Athletic Club. Horse meat cuts included T-bone, sirloin, and pot roast.

It wasn't long before charges were made of a black market in meat in both St. Louis and East St. Louis. The OPA saw such "outlaw activities" as "a menace to health and the national price structure." Public health officials pointed out that black market meat could transmit tuberculosis, rabies, and undulant fever.

The *Star Times* said that March 26, the day before meat rationing began, saw "the greatest meat-buying rush in the history of St. Louis." Butcher shops were swamped. At A. Moll Grocery Store, 5659 Delmar, 500 customer numbers were given out before noon. People took anything, including balogna. The next day the OPA authorized 1,500,000 more pounds of meat for St. Louis. Area packers — Krey, Hunter, Laclede, American, Sieloff, Heil, and St. Louis Independent — struggled to keep up with the demand.

Ironically, as soon as rationing began, surplus meat piled up and had to be sold at a discount because it was in danger of spoiling. Customers who had loaded up the week before were not in a hurry to use up their precious ration points. Some 200,000 pounds of sausage went begging because the point value was too high — it equaled that of round steak. Ceiling prices were set at 38 cents a pound for roast beef, 46 cents for sirloin steak, 62 cents for porterhouse steak, and 31 cents for hamburger. Each person received sixteen points per week to buy rationed meats, fats, and cheese. Kosher meats had a special point value system.

At 2 P.M. Sunday, March 21, the OPA announced over the radio that the sale of butter, lard, margarine, shortening, and cooking oil would be frozen at midnight. By 2:30, stores were packed with customers. Many stayed open as late as midnight, trying to serve everyone who wanted to stock up before the freeze began. Pevely and St. Louis dairies sold completely out of dairy products.

Cheese rationing was tied to meat rationing — the same coupons could be used for either. Two hundred and fifty kinds of cheese were not rationed, including cream, cottage, camembert, brie, and bleu. But the most popular cheeses were: American, cheddar, grated Parmesan, gouda, edam, brick, Swiss, and muenster. Each pound required surrendering eight rationing points.

Other dairy products were not rationed, but were scarce, especially milk, cream, and ice cream. All milk products had to be ordered well in advance from milkmen. Last-minute notes stuck in milk bottles pleading for an extra quart of milk were no longer honored. Anheuser-Busch vice president James J. Carroll and his wife, who lived at 15 Kingsbury Place, were so frustrated by shortages they bought a cow. Carroll wanted cream in his coffee and couldn't get it at the store. The cow, named Hi-Hat, gave four gallons of milk daily.

The OPA ended bread slicing shortly after the first of the the year as a way to increase production. Even packaged breads came unsliced. The experiment ended March 8 because it turned out to be more trouble for large bakeries not to slice bread than to slice it. Local bakers were restricted to selling three kinds of bread and nine kinds of buns and rolls. Violators were subject to fine or imprisonment. Because of such regulations and because of shortages of ingredients and manpower, about one-fourth of the small bakeries in the area closed.

With the beginning of spring, the food crisis continued to look grim. Food administrator Claude R. Wickard and War Manpower Commission chief Paul V. McNutt announced that 3,500,000 more people were needed on the farms to produce enough food for America. Wickard emphasized that the situation was much worse than most people realized. Thousands of young farmers had enlisted in the military — even though they could get deferments — or had headed for high-paying defense jobs in the cities, leaving women and children to operate the farms. Most managed very well, but couldn't keep up with

A gridiron skit presented by the Women's Advertising Club looked at the silver lining surrounding rationed food. Mary Lee Twitch, "the expert who knows how to stretch everything except a war-time girdle," of the OCD Nutrition Council gave some pointers to her audience:

Good morning, homemakers! I know what problems you're up against these days — trying to think of new ways to stretch your ration points . . . really, with just a little imagination it's absolutely ASTOUNDING what you can do with rationed foods.

Take butter, for example — I take it every chance I get, which isn't often. This morning I have a perfectly hideous recipe for butter spread . . . that makes a whole POUND of spread out of just one stick. Now here's what you do. First you take the stick — so — and put it into your mixing bowl. Add a small jar of vaseline — that's not rationed, you know, and it has the same smooth texture that butter has. Then stir in a package of gelatin . . . — and finally, a can of Pet Milk! Mix together thoroughly — and ladies, you'll be SURPRISED at what you get!

Tomorrow I'll tell you about a perfectly enchanting recipe for Corn Chowder that doesn't take a single kernel of corn. You just heat your water — then grind up a few front pages of the *Globe-Democrat* and mix them in slowly to give your chowder that rich corn flavor. Simple, isn't it?

Now one more hint before I go. There are all kinds of ways to stretch meat, but the best way, I think, is to take a slice of braunsweiger and press it gently between two telephone directories. Let it stand for a few seconds — and almost before you know it, you'll have enough braunsweiger to make three big sandwiches! Later, of course, you can use the telephone directories for making soup — to give your soup that good meat flavor.

the demand.

To help out, St. Louis area meat cutters volunteered to butcher animals on nearby farms on their days off. About 1,200 high school and college students also signed up to work on area farms. Their average daily pay was $1 plus board and room, if they had to spend the night. Most students worked in St. Louis County and their chores included sowing, cultivating, harvesting, picking berries, packing fruits and vegetables, and canning. The most practical solution to the food crisis was the victory garden. Much more than a hobby for a dilettante,

Two hundred quarts of produce were canned from this garden owned and cultivated by Mr. and Mrs. Alex Hihn, Elmo's grandparents.

Five-year-old Elmo Hihn, Jr., with the harvest from his victory garden.

the victory garden kept families supplied with necessary food. Across the nation, victory gardens produced millions of dollars worth of crops. In the St. Louis area, some 35,000 gardens harvested an average of twenty bushels of fruit and vegetables each. Good growing weather in June and July brought an especially rich bounty to many area gardens.

One outstanding garden project with 102 plots sprouted on Skinker Boulevard, between Rosebury and Northwood. An organizer of the project, Sidney Landau, said, "We don't allow any food to waste. If we can't eat it, we give it away, and we don't allow any plot to remain uncultivated. If anyone loses interest in his plot, there is a waiting list eager to carry on."

Perhaps the most important part of gardening was the canning and preserving of the harvest, which could provide a family with fruit and vegetables all year. To the great frustration of homemakers, a shortage of canning supplies developed in late summer and once again, they were forced to wait in line and settle for less than enough. A consequence both of home canning and the rationing of canned goods was that fewer tin cans were available for the scrap drives.

In the middle of a July heat wave, just as the meat shortage was easing, another critical shortage developed — beer. Perhaps to compensate for leaving thousands of St. Louisans hot and thirsty, Anheuser-

Newspaper cartoonist Vic Vac illustrated the happy situation of the city's shoemakers. They had more work than they could handle once shoe rationing began.

Busch began producing synthetic meat, a sausage made of yeast, high-protein cereals and molasses. It was compared to steak in nutritional value, but not in taste. However one newspaper account reported that "it wasn't half bad."

Shoe rationing began the first week in February. As with all other rationing, sales were halted a few days before rationing was to begin, but first customers were allowed one last buying spree. It was ironic that a shoe shortage could exist in St. Louis, the second largest shoe-producing area in the nation. But St. Louis shoe manufacturers, among them Brown, International, Johansen, and Wohl, were turning out millions of pairs of military boots and shoes. Civilian shoes were low priority.

On February 9 rationing stamp #7 was issued, which was earmarked for shoes. At once OPA undercover agents began to test the system and within ten days, Srenco Shoe Store was charged with selling a pair of shoes without a coupon. On June 14, the last day that coupon #7 was redeemable, shoe stores were swamped. Stamp #8 replaced #17, but by then local shoe stores were so depleted that they couldn't fill new orders.

The production of paper products was also curtailed, but they were not rationed. After January 9 there were no more paper drapes, fireworks, paper shirt protectors, paper hats for birthdays or New Year's Eve, liquor packaging, photograph albums, shelf paper, place cards, paper aprons, paper flowers, or cardboard poker chips.

Attempting to enforce rationing procedures gave the city a colossal headache. The rules for gasoline rationing stated that the correct sticker must be on the windshield and the correct coupon be shown the attendant before gas could be pumped. Each coupon had to be endorsed on the back with the owner's driver's license number. The coupons could be used only during stipulated times and were invalid after their expiration date.

Each one of the rules was violated to a greater or lesser degree. The most common offense was that the driver "forgot" the necessary coupons, making the attendant a villain if he wouldn't pump a little gas anyway. But if the attendant agreed to be a good guy and overlook the infraction, the station was liable for stiff penalties. When drivers were caught in an infraction, their coupon books could be revoked, which in effect took away their cars. Drivers charged with speeding, carelessness, or driving while intoxicated could also lose their coupon books. One filling station operator admitted to counterfeiting 3,000 A coupons which he had hoped to sell. A printer turned him in before that could happen.

A *Star-Times* survey in late March showed that only four of 140 gas stations were selling gasoline without coupons. In June officials began noting license plate numbers of cars parked at Fairmont Raceway. Later, odometers of the cars were checked to see if drivers were violating gas rationing regulations, since visiting the racetrack was "non-essential."

Coffee rationing was also frustrating. Seven downtown coffee shops, mainly in hotels, and Miss Hulling's Cafeteria were accused of violating coffee rationing regulations in mid-January. They were supposed to make periodic reports of the amount of coffee that they had on hand and when they did so, discrepancies were uncovered. The ruling came about a month later — the guilty cafes with excess coffee had to turn in their coupons. The Lennox, Mayfair, and Warwick hotels agreed to surrender their coupons without a fight.

One shortage popped up that was totally unexpected. The St. Louis Police Department ran out of buttons. Brass was unavailable except to the military. The department issued an appeal to the community for old buttons, and the story was carried nationally by the wire services. A Connecticut firm with a reserve of police buttons came to the rescue.

On February 26 the first blackout of the year was held. It was ninety-nine percent effective and CD director McBride was "elated." All street and alley lights went out at once and so did the lights in industrial

The prototype of the C-46 Curtiss Commando was manufactured in St. Louis and named for this city.

plants (except for those with blackout curtains), buses, streetcars, automobiles, and trains. Four of the twelve districts were 100 percent dark.

To add drama to the blackout, four targets were designated as bombed — an apartment building at 5475 Cabanne Avenue, St. Anthony's High School, the intersection of Meramec and Michigan streets, and the Krey Packing Company. No one knew in advance where the "enemy" was going to strike. The response of ambulances and first aid teams, fire fighters and demolition experts to the simulated emergency sites was reported to be immediate and professional.

Shortly after the blackout, a group of air raid wardens decided to "take a walk," from a strategy meeting at Mason School, because the room they were given was too small to work in. "We were shoved off in a little playroom," said one disgruntled warden. "We just can't work there." The principal countered with charges that the wardens had left the gym littered with cigarette butts after their last meeting and the dispute ended in a standoff.

Defense production peaked in 1943 in St. Louis; over 200,000 workers were employed in war plants here. The "underemployed" — blacks, women, the over-forty worker — continued to be courted. Many returning veterans were given jobs in defense factories. Over 6,500 veterans returned from the war in 1943. Some 400 of them had been wounded, many with disabling injuries. The handicapped were proving to be extremely able workers. Busch-Sulzer hired several who had been partially paralyzed by polio. Deaf trainees were taught production skills at McDonnell Aircraft, and at Mines Equipment Company blind persons manufactured and packed repair kits for cables used by the army signal corps. "They see with their fingers," said production manager J. E. Miller.

In February, when the War Manpower Commission announced that a forty-eight hour week would become standard for centers of defense production, Col. Henry Scullin of Scullin Steel laughed. Most defense plants in St. Louis, he pointed out, had been working a forty-eight hour week for some time, and Curtiss-Wright was on a sixty-hour week.

The aircraft company was the glamour plant among St. Louis defense industries, employing 11,000 workers at its peak. The Curtiss C-46 Commando, originally planned as a luxury airliner, had been redesigned as a cargo plane with extra-wide doors. The largest twin-engine transport in the world, it could carry 15,000 pounds of supplies on a 1,000-mile flight and could tow gliders at the same time. It was also the only U.S. transport plane to make it "over the hump," across the Himalaya Mountains to China, said to be the most treacherous stretch of airspace in the war. Since the Commando was designed here, its prototype was called *St. Louis.* Production, however, was in the Buffalo, New York, plant until late in 1943, when it shifted to St. Louis. During the invasion of 1944, Commandos carried paratroopers and supplies to the Continent.

Curtiss-Wright had been designing and testing dive-bombers since 1928. Its Helldiver (SB2C) was credited with being the fastest and most deadly of its species. Its wings could be folded, allowing two planes to be carried at a time on an aircraft carrier elevator. The bomb load was completely enclosed within its fuselage. One giant bomb or two smaller ones could be carried in the bomb bay. The plane's design gave the gunner excellent visibility for a wide field of fire.

In May an experimental Curtiss-Wright plane made of plywood, the C-76 Caravan, fell apart in midair over Louisville, Kentucky. One of St. Louis' favorite pilots was killed in the accident. An aviation pioneer, Duke Trowbridge had been chief pilot for Robertson Aircraft for years.

Mainly because of Curtiss-Wright and St. Louis Aircraft Corporation, which turned out over 700 training planes (PT-19s and PT-23s) for the military, St. Louis was considered part of the midwestern aircraft production "triangle," along with Kansas City and Wichita, Kansas, where Boeing made the giant B-29 bombers. These "Superfortresses" were a key ingredient in the formula for victory. During

Helldiver Squadron (Dodd, Mead & Co., 1944) chronicles the exploits of a team of navy fliers in the Pacific. The following excerpt tells of a mission run by Lt. (jg) Jesse Bristow of St. Louis and John Lawrence, ARMC 2C, of Springfield, Massachusetts.

Briss Bristow and Sig Sigman got separated from the others during the approach. Sig finally landed aboard another carrier and joined a later strike. . . . When Briss came down through the clouds he found himself flying through heavy AA and diving toward the sea.

"That was pretty lousy," Briss said sourly to his gunner, Johnny Lawrence. He pulled back up into the clouds. "Do you want to go back, Johnny?"

"Yes, sir, Mr. Bristow," said Johnny. "We've still got our bomb."

"Okay," said Briss. "Here goes nothing."

The lone Helldiver popped through the clouds. Ack-ack converged quickly, but already the bomb was on its way and Briss' forward guns cut a swath through the winking AA guns. Johnny saw the bomb hit and something burst into flames, then he was busy strafing everything in sight as the bomber sped eastward over the island. The sun was just coming up. Briss turned and saw the beginning of the end of a pretty tropical island. Two large fires were burning on the northwest coast of Betio.

1944 and 1945 they mercilessly bombed Germany and Japan until finally the enemy's resources to continue the fight were gone.

McDonnell Aircraft Company was one of twelve St. Louis subcontractors for the Superfortress. McDonnell produced only one entire airplane during the war that was accepted by the Army Air Force, a P-67. The company worked primarily on developing experimental jet aircraft, which did not come into their own until after the war.

Perhaps the best-known supplier of compenents for military aircraft in the area was Emerson Electric Company. Emerson was commissioned by the Army Air Corps in 1940 to investigate the British production of machine gun turrets for bombers. While in England president Stuart Symington picked up several innovative ideas which he brought back to St. Louis for his engineers to refine. They developed the model ANB gun turret, which evolved through the next few years into several electrically-controlled models and won the praises of gunners stationed all over the world. One fan wrote to the company, "Emerson turrets are doing a whale of a job for us and the Huns have felt their sting many times. Keep building turrets for us and we'll do the job."

*The navy's SB2C Helldiver dive **bomber** was manufactured at the Curtiss-Wright plant near Lambert Field.*

Emerson turrets were designed primarily for the B-17 Flying Fortress and the B-24 Liberator. At the height of production, the company built six different turrets on six assembly lines. Emerson also produced high-speed electric aircraft motors for bomber and fighter controls. Alco Valve Company, a subsidiary of Emerson, made control valves for combat planes, hydraulic aircraft controls, and radio direction finders for medium and heavy bombers. American Stove Company (best known as makers of Magic Chef ranges) made auxiliary gasoline tanks for fighter escorts. Presstite provided the sealants for those tanks and for the pressurized cabins of the Superfortresses; Essmueller and Owens-Illinois Glass Company worked on bombsights for aircraft, and McQuay-Norris turned out piston rings for aircraft engines.

Alcoa provided sheet metal for airplanes and National Foundry & Machine Company did the castings. Thomas J. White Company produced the molded floors for B-24s by laminating eighty-one sheets of paper. The resulting floor was stronger and lighter than a metal one. S. G. Adams Company made instrument panels for the P-47 Thunderbolt, and Independent Engineering Company won an "E" for producing oxygen cylinders for high-flying aircraft. Independent Engineering also made high-pressure hydrogen generators for Army Air Corps barrage balloons, which were designed to impede incoming German rockets. St. Louis Aircraft Company made balloon gondolas for the army.

St. Louis Aircraft assembly line turned out a steady stream of PT-23 trainers in 1943 at the height of production.

The PT-23, assembled at St. Louis Aircraft Company.

Courtesy Gregory M. Franzwa

TBM Avengers, the navy's torpedo bombers, used Emerson Electric gun turrets.

The turret-painting group at Emerson Electric gave Roy Pendleton a shower when he became a father.

Although most of the area's contribution to the war effort was in equipment for destruction, much of it was in medical supplies. The St. Louis Army Medical Depot, located in the Mart Building, was one of the largest such operations in the nation. Field hospitals were equipped there and shipped out all over the globe. In February alone 35,000,000 pounds of medical supplies and equipment were sent to GIs wherever they were stationed. Since quinine supplies were no longer available, atabrine tablets were used to combat malaria and "whole handfuls" of sulfa drugs were poured on wounds to fight infection. But in spite of the emerging miracle drugs — antibiotics were just then coming into their own — the most frequently requested drug was still aspirin. And Monsanto Chemical Company produced most of that for all the armed forces.

Many kinds of drugs were supplied to the services by Monsanto, Lambert Pharmacal Company, (both won an "E" for their contributions) and Heil Corporation. Heil also produced surgical supplies, and Absorbent Cotton Company was awarded an "E" for the excellence of its surgical dressings. Several garment factories, including Forest City Manufacturing Company, produced nurses' uniforms, surgical gowns, and bedding for the Medical Department. Koken Companies made a

Wagner Electric Company's sprawling Wellston plant made brakes for military vehicles.

Presstite sealants were used in land vehicles as well as in aircraft. In March 1945 the company received a letter from an enthusiastic GI:

One day in the Aleutians we drove our tank upstream until it was in water up to the turret. We went through five feet of water and flooded the fighting compartment, but the motor kept turning over and enabled us to pull out of the stream. Our driver had so much water inside him that he ''stalled'' on us for about five minutes while he choked and sputtered, and we drained water out of the tank for two minutes, but the engine kept turning over smoothly. Too bad you don't make a sealing compound to be used on the drivers.

unique contribution to medical care with their specially-made operating tables for horses in the cavalry. The company also made examining tables for humans.

Hundreds of St. Louis doctors and nurses shipped out with the troops. Several graduating classes of nurses enlisted as a unit in the armed forces, causing a critical nurse shortage in local hospitals. Volunteers and nurse's aides took up the slack as well as they could.

The 21st General Hospital, sponsored by Barnes Hospital, was sent to Sidi Ben Hanifa in North Africa on Christmas Eve in 1942. There it converted a group of resort hotels into medical facilities. About 4,000 wounded men from the Tunis-Bizerte battles were sent to the

The John Nooter Boiler Works fabricated the vats that allowed for the incubation of life-saving penicillin.

1,000-bed hospital, straining its resources to the breaking point. Commanded by Lt. Col. Lee D. Cady, former president of the St. Louis Medical Society, the 21st moved to Naples in 1943, where it cared primarily for patients with infectious diseases. It also inaugurated a reconditioning physical therapy program for convalescent patients which was later adopted by other military hospitals.

Saint Louis University sponsored the 70th General Hospital, which was assigned to Assi Bou Nif, also in North Africa, in 1943. Although planned as a long-term, permanent hospital, the unit was quartered in primitive tents, which were surprisingly chilly at night according to reports. Col. Curtis H. Lohr, the former superintendent of St. Louis County Hospital, commanded the 70th, and Rev. Harry B. Crimmins, S.J., resigned as president of Saint Louis University to act as its chaplain. In January 1944 the hospital moved to Pistoia, Italy, to care for those wounded in the Italian campaign. The surgical load was extremely heavy.

Lohr told a reporter in the spring of 1945, "There were times when battle casualties pouring in kept us working 48 hours at a stretch. Plasma, whole blood, penicillin and the sulfonamides performed wonders. We get whole blood from our own personnel, particularly when we need a certain type, and from troops in the neighborhood."

Probably the greatest boon to convalescence was the use of penicillin, which cut the time needed for recovery dramatically. At Saint Louis University's School of Medicine, Dr. Edward A. Doisy worked practically around the clock to isolate penicillin B, which was many times more powerful than penicillin A. His discovery was immediately used by the military.

Penicillin was easily grown in small amounts by 1942, but mass production was a long way from realization until John Nooter Boiler Works of St. Louis devised 20,000-gallon tanks that were successfully used for its cultivation. In 1943 enough penicillin was available to treat

Presenting the Army-Navy "E" award for production of war materials to officials of Nooter Boiler Works are (left) Lt. Col. Richard W. Coward, executive officer of the St. Louis Ordnance District, and (right) Lt. Cmdr. M. K. Arenberg, assistant supervisor of shipbuilding in St. Louis. Receiving the award are from left: Robert J. Ryan, then general manager of the firm; Elmer J. Nooter, vice president; and Harry Nooter, president.

thirty to forty people a month; by 1944 there was enough to treat 7,000 people each day.

As great numbers of convalescing GIs returned to the states, army bases couldn't hold them all. A convalescent camp for soldiers from Jefferson Barracks Hospital was established at Babler State Park, west of the city. It boasted an occupational therapy program, which was the first of its kind in the United States.

Almost ninety-eight percent of American troops wounded in the war survived, an incredible percentage. Still, that meant that two percent did not survive. Families at home dreaded the sound of a doorbell ringing or the sight of a Western Union messenger on his bicycle. Gold stars in windows announced a death; silver stars marked the home of wounded vet. "Get the boys home!" was an unsung refrain that rang through everyone's mind. Home, and safe.

The Second War Loan Drive campaign opened on March 12. St. Louis had been the first major city to go over the top in the first drive and had been rewarded by a place as the lead float in the 1943 Parade

St. Louisan Willa Corse, right, was one of four WACS who modeled regulation uniforms in Washington, D.C.

of Bonds, renamed from the Tournament of Roses, in Pasadena, California. The feeling in the city was, "let's do it again." Campaign chairman Chapin S. Newhard, a stock broker, gave the city a pep talk. "We want to be not only the first large city over the top, but we have raised our sights and are shooting for two other marks," he said. "We want to oversubscribe our quota more than any other city, and we want to have the greatest number of individual purchases in proportion to population."

Four days later eighty-nine percent of the goal had been reached. The Missouri Pacific Railroad alone had purchased twenty million dollars worth of bonds. Boy Scout Louis M. Bohnenkamp of Kirkwood High School was credited with selling $200,000 in bonds to MoPac treasurer Edwin G. Wagner. By the fifth day of the drive, St. Louis did go over the top, the first large city to do so. A few days later it reached the hundred million dollar mark and then surpassed that.

Newhard and Walter H. Head, president of General American Life Insurance Company and deputy chairman of the drive, congratulated each other on their success. "The people did it," said Newhard. "It was a crusade, a spontaneous upsurge of the people."

An unidentified Red Cross volunteer driver prepares to move a jeep from the army transportation depot on North Broadway.

Intense concentration sometimes was required of production workers.

Only about sixteen percent of the registered voters voted in the local election on April 6. They elected aldermen, school board members, and delegates to the state constitutional convention. One of the alderman elected was Rev. Jasper C. Caston, the first black to serve on the board. Another was Clara Hempelmann, the city's first woman alderman.

When interviewed about the future of women in politics, Hempelmann said, "They are just pioneering, but they are coming into their own. We are living in a changing world, and women today are doing things they never had to do before, not only in politics, but in every other field.

"Very few women in politics have yet had the courage to go out and ask to be elected. I think my election is proof that any woman who has political ambitions — and the courage to act upon them — has nothing to fear at the hands of the voters."

The first woman weather forecasters at Lambert Field, the first woman zoo attendant and the first woman streetcar conductor appeared in 1943. Women interns at City Hospital outnumbered men for the first time in history. St. Louis women enlisted in the newly established SPARs (Coast Guard) and Women's Marine Corps.

WAVEs were assigned to duty at the Naval Air Station at Lambert, and WAACs were sent to Jefferson Barracks — the first time women had been allowed to stay within its walls since its founding in 1826. (The Barracks band played "Hail, Hail, The Gang's All Here" when the WAACs arrived.) Olympic medalist and track star Helen Stephens traded in her running shoes for a defense job at Curtiss-Wright. Almost three-fourths of the production staff at U.S. Cartridge was female by mid-1943, and the need for more women workers everywhere was so acute that there was talk of undertaking a door-to-door search for them.

In July when it was announced that fathers would be drafted and the work force depleted even further, machines and workers were transported to Stix Baer and Fuller for a "hands on" demonstration fair. Women could wander through a mock-up of a defense plant and learn about welding or operating lathes, manufacturing piston rings, or assembling airfoil surface subassemblies. An employment recruiter stood by, waiting to sign up anyone who showed an interest.

Women in voluntary war work combined their efforts and formed the Women's War Council. Florine Magruder presided over the council, which included members of the Red Cross, American Women Volunteers in Service, USO, and OCD. The USO was constantly pleading for refreshments, needing 12,000 cookies each weekend at the Municipal Auditorium center alone.

Rosemary Kehler decided to put her skills to use for the war effort and organized the "Keep 'Em Flying Knitting Unit of South St. Louis." She enlisted thirty-five pairs of knitting needles (and their owners). Together the group made socks, turtleneck sweaters, gloves, helmet liners, and scarves for servicemen. They outfitted St. Louisan Herbert Harrison, who had survived the sinking of the *Yorktown,* but had lost all his clothes.

April 20 marked Adolf Hitler's fifty-fourth birthday. The Women's Ad Club decided that was an event that should be commemorated with appropriate fanfare and planned "the last birthday party ever for Adolf Schicklgruber." Much of the city joined in the celebration. Carl's Bar at 709 Washington offered a special Blood and Thunder cocktail to say "Here's mud in your eye, Adolf!"

Gifts to Adolf were collected at Kiel Auditorium — war bonds, money for the Red Cross war fund, blood, scrap metal, grease and fat. An auction at the birthday party brought in $57,000 for war bonds. Chamber of Commerce president Thomas N. Dysart bought a nightgown which had belonged to movie star Gertrude Lawrence for $2,000 and gave it to Chapin S. Newhard, chairman of the second war bond drive with a note: "Let this be a bond between us." An autographed record of Kate Smith's "God Bless America" was auctioned off (despite being cracked) along with Wendell Willkie's autographed best selling book *One World* and a twelve-pound rib roast, which went for $1,000.

Contralto Marian Anderson came to St. Louis in March to sing at the Municipal Auditorium. Her contribution to the war effort, she said, was to fight "hate and prejudice and heartache." She hoped that listeners at her concert would not notice the color of her face, but would see only her soul. "And that," she said, " is colorless." The concert, a sellout, was called magnificent and glorious. At the same time that Marian Anderson was in town, former St. Louisan Josephine Baker was wowing black American troops in North Africa with her dancing.

Dozens of celebrities visited the city to inspire defense workers to greater levels of production. Mr. and Mrs. Thomas F. Sullivan of Waterloo, Iowa, were among them. The Sullivan's five sons, "the fighting Sullivans," had been lost in the sinking of the cruiser *Juneau* off Guadalcanal in the desperate battle there in the fall of 1942.

The "Jack-the-Ripper" Flying Fortress crew came to St. Louis a few weeks after the Sullivans' visit to spur production. Its crew of ten men had participated in eleven bombing missions in Europe. The plane had been riddled with flak and machine gun bullets and two engines had been shot away, but the crew managed to land safely. They told their story over and over as they visited Curtiss-Wright, McDonnell, McQuay-Norris, Emerson Electric, and U.S. Cartridge.

In July the "Flying Dutchmen," came to town in conjunction with a Dutch art exhibit at the Art Museum. These gallant pilots flew from a British air base to fight the Luftwaffe over their Nazi-occupied country.

The most famous visitor to come through St. Louis in 1943 was the commander-in-chief himself. On April 27 President Roosevelt took a surprise forty-seven-minute tour of Jefferson Barracks and reviewed 15,000 troops, including WAACs. His train then passed by Union Station on its way east, but he did not stop in the city. His visit was a well-kept secret and the news was not released until he was on his way home.

However, someone knew Roosevelt was coming. A few days before his visit, troops at the barracks were drilled until they almost dropped. Floors and walls were scrubbed down to the wood. A reporter commented, "When the President arrived, the aroma of shoe polish pervaded the barracks, buttons glistened, and the hair of every soldier was slickened to patent leather smoothness."

On April 21 Forest Park was "attacked" in a sudden blitzkreig by troops from Jefferson Barracks. The park was cleared of civilians in thirty minutes and bombs "destroyed" the old mounted police station, the Art Museum, the Muni Opera theater, administration building

A mock Sicilian Village was a target during the Battle of Art Hill in Forest Park.

and picnic grounds. Five Boy Scouts from St. Roch's School were designated as "trapped" at the mounted police station and evacuated through the coal chute. Unhurt, they were sent as part of the drill to a hospital in ambulances with sirens screaming, an experience that they found exhilarating.

In January Franklin Roosevelt had said in his State of the Union address, "we are going to strike and strike hard." Apparently United Mine Workers president John L. Lewis was listening. On April 27 26,000 coal miners walked off their jobs. The strike spread. By May 1, when 41,000 miners in Illinois were idle, Roosevelt ordered Harold Ickes, secretary of the interior, to take over the mines and to send soldiers into the pits. At Peabody Coal Company almost a half-million miners refused to go into the mines.

In St. Louis Harold Gibbons, director of the St. Louis Joint Council of CIO, protested against the use of American troops in the coal mines and claimed that 4,500 CIO workers in the area supported the United Mine Workers. But a few days later members of the St. Louis CIO board announced that they were backing the no-strike vow taken by labor unions at the beginning of the war and denounced the stand taken by Lewis and Gibbons. Their statement, written for the signatures of individual members, read,

"I am not going to break my no-strike pact with the President of the United States of America. I should not like to have it said about American labor that you or I leaned over the dying body of an

American soldier and said, 'Son, you wouldn't be dying today if I had done my job back home.' This issue is bigger than any of the petty things over which we struggle in the United States today because on the outcome depends the future of freedom of the world.''

The CIO executive board continued, ''We disassociate ourselves from the acts and statements of any CIO member or officer who gives support to John L. Lewis in his acts against the war effort and the welfare of the American workers.''

''During the strike American Communist Earl Browder appeared at Kiel Auditorium. Speaking to about a thousand people, he also attacked Lewis' strike policy and drew heavy applause. Browder had kind words for Philip Murray, president of the CIO, who advocated the cooperation of labor and management for the duration.

Only two days after Browder vacated the podium at Kiel, Murray himself took it over and spoke to a huge, enthusiastic crowd. He was in town for the the eight-state AAUW-CIO conference which was held at the Hotel Jefferson. There labor leaders reaffirmed the importance of producing defense materiel without work stoppages.

But even as they were discussing the need for a commitment to full production, across town at the St. Louis ordnance plant, thirty whites were refusing to work because a black had been promoted to floor man. Three weeks later, 3,600 blacks walked off the job because they objected to the presence of a white foreman in a black unit. Plant management used arguments based on such disputes to keep the races segregated.

Shortly after the coal miners strike began in May, Lewis agreed to a fifteen-day ''truce'' and told miners to go back to work while contract details were being worked out. The truce collapsed on the first of June and again miners stayed out of the mines. In Illinois 200 mines were shut down. The strike spread throughout the country and by mid-June, virtually the entire coal industry had come to a halt.

St. Louis War Dads wrote a public letter to President Roosevelt in protest of the mines' closing and PFC Vincent Hug wrote home from his machine gun battery in the Far East his opinion of the striking miners: ''I wish to hell they would send some of [them] to be guards over here. I'll bet that after about two days they would be glad to return to work.''

May was a month of unusually heavy rains. As was often the case, that meant flooding of the Meramec, Missouri, and Mississippi rivers. St. Louisans noticed with suprise that some of the men sandbagging the Mississippi riverbank near Ste. Genevieve were wearing blue jackets stenciled with the letters ''P-W.'' Armed soldiers guarded them. For the first time the city became aware that prisoners of war were being interned nearby. Italian prisoners of war were held in Weingarten, Missouri, with others at Fort Leonard Wood and Camp Clark. Germans were kept in the vicinity of Jefferson Barracks, but most Nazi prisoners were kept at Fort Chaffee in Arkansas. (In June 1943 almost 37,000 Axis prisoners were interned in the United States at twenty-one locations.)

Despite the vigorous work by POWs, troops from Jefferson Barracks and Scott Field, school children, and anyone else who would wield a shovel or toss a sandbag, the river won in 1943. Some 200,000 acres of rich Missouri farmland just sprouting from the spring planting were innundated. With food already in short supply, the flood seemed a disaster. There were mutterings about a coming famine. But despite the critical shortage of farm labor, crops were replanted by the first of June.

The thirteen straight days of rain meant that some streets in the city and suburbs were under water and railroad tracks were washing out. Rising water at the St. Louis ordnance depot, 7140 N. Broadway, sent hundreds of jeeps, ambulances, and trucks to higher ground.

In mid-May a political trial briefly made front-page news. David D. Erwin and General Lee Butler were tried in East St. Louis for conspiracy to violate the wartime sedition act. During the 1930s a Filipino masquerading as a Japanese had approached several black groups in the St. Louis area urging them to form an organization called the Pacific Movement of the Eastern World. It was alleged that in June 1939, Erwin, now a member of the organization, had said that the Japanese were "the champions of the dark and colored people."

When the FBI arrested Butler in September 1942 they found a rifle with 400 rounds of ammunition in his possession and two suspicious books — *Travel Comforts in Japan* and *Visit Japan*. There was also a black, brown, red, and yellow flag which was said to represent the "Triumphant Church of the New Age." One month after the trial began, it ended. Erwin was sentenced to four years in prison for being the "intellectual leader" of a seditious group, and Butler was sentenced to two years. George L. Vaughn, the chief defense counsel, promised an appeal.

St. Louisans enjoyed spending the money they earned in defense plants. "Assuming money talks," said one merchant, "then the rush to spend money and to spend it hard, fast, good, and often, can be likened to a veritable Niagara Falls roar of dollar sounds." Perfume at $45 an ounce, five-dollar ties, fur coats, caviar, and other luxuries evaporated on payday. Deposits in St. Louis banks surpassed one billion dollars for the first time ever in July, and the 8th Federal Reserve District announced that seventeen billion dollars were in circulation here, four billion more than in 1942.

One way that soldiers, sailors, marines, WAVES and SPARS spent

After the lean years of the depression, the war years brought long lines of depositors to savings tellers and a welcome prosperity to St. Louisans.

their money was to visit Bert Grimm in his tattoo parlor on North Broadway. A woman customer at a Bert's downtown tattoo parlor asked Bert to change the motto "Death Before Dishonor" to "Death Before Dishwashing." Another customer, in a burst of good feeling for America's Chinese allies, brought in a a piece of paper with the Chinese characters for "Good luck, farewell!" for Bert to copy onto his body. Later he found out the characters actually spelled out "four pairs socks, two suits underwear, five handkerchiefs."

Whether soldier, sailor, or civilian, St. Louisans who wanted to have a good time on the town headed for their favorite night spots. Eddie ("Careless") Howard pulled the over-twenty-one crowd into Tune Town and so did Little Jack Little, Ella Fitzgerald, Les Brown and Sunny Dunham, Stan Kenton, Herb Mahler and Jack Fields. The over-thirty crowd preferred the Showboat Ballroom on Delmar where they did the "pump handle" waltz to songs like "My Buddy."

Serious jitterbuggers ("hoppers") went to Casa Loma or Forest Park Highlands, where they had enough room to really swing. The Highlands, just south of Forest Park on Oakland, offered a full amusement park and giant swimming pool. Name bands like Fats Waller, Ted Lewis, and Lawrence Welk, were paid up to $3,000 per week to entertain the crowds.

As the summer of 1943 came to St. Louis, temperatures, humidity, and tempers rose. The army had first call on freon, which it used as an

Courtesy Jim Eisenbeis

Sailors enjoying liberty at the Casa Loma ballroom, at 3354 Iowa Avenue in south St. Louis.

Tony Sansone, in his zoot suit, and Frances Mahoney jitterbug for their fans at the 826 Club in the basement of Pilgrim Congregational Church.

insecticide, resulting in a shortage for air conditioning units. Workers in downtown office buildings and stores sweltered through June, July, and August as thermostats were set to seventy-eight degrees. (Air conditioning was not in widespread use at the time, but many downtown buildings had some sort of cooling system.)

In Detroit on June 20 summer tensions flared into one of the worst race riots of all time, as mobs of whites invaded black residential areas, killing, burning, and looting. Thirty-four people were killed, millions of dollars in damages were inflicted, and one million man-hours were lost to defense production. St. Louis leaders, eyeing the racial situation here nervously, formed a race relations council, spearheaded by the CIO. When a race riot erupted in Harlem a few weeks later, St. Louis businessmen, clergy, and politicians began to think hard about ways to avoid racial violence.

On the Fourth of July, as on every other holiday, "Don't travel!" pleas were heard and ignored. Goverment officials hoped to keep transporation open for the great numbers of servicemen and women. Buses and trains were jammed and the city was thronged with crowds. People lined up all the way into Eighteenth Street to ride Missouri Pacific's "Sunshine Special," and cots were squeezed into every available space at downtown hotels. On Saturday night of the holiday weekend, the first-ever night major league baseball game was played at Sportsman's Park: the Browns vs. the Washington Senators. Moolah Temple Shriners sponsored a fireworks display at the public school stadium.

The Italian campaign heated up in mid-July. Sicily was invaded on July 10, and from there Allied troops gradually battled their way to the mainland. On July 26 with the government collapsing around him, Benito Mussolini resigned as dictator. In St. Louis, baseball fans at Sportsman's Park cheered long and loud when they heard of his resignation. On the Hill, the celebrating went on for hours. "It is the end of facism," said a jubilant Samuel Chinici, operator of a gas station on Shaw. Earlier in the year, an Italian-American organization had called Mussolini, "the darkest demon from the lowest depths of hell." When Italy surrendered on September 8, the Hill was alive with joyous, jubilant celebrations. In the 5200 block of Wilson alone, fifty sons were serving in uniform.

In the Pacific during the summer U.S. forces continued their strategy of island-hopping, moving ever closer to Japan. On July 12 and 13, during the second battle of Kula Gulf, the light cruiser *St. Louis* was torpedoed, but survived the battle. (In fact, she returned after repairs to set a new naval gunfire record in a later battle.) The *St. Louis,* like the *Nashville, Montpelier,* and *Cleveland,* was part of task force HOW under Admiral William F. Halsey. She was present at the attack on Munda Point and provided covering support for ships going "up the slot" between the Solomon Islands.

Mayor William Dee Becker at age 66 was a balding, somewhat pudgy man. Affable, accessible and fairly honest, Becker was called "reasonably competent" by the *Star-Times* and most people said he wasn't a bad mayor and that was something to be grateful for. A Republican, Becker was miles away from his predecessor, the dynamic New Dealer Bernard F. Dickmann. Dickmann had tried to change St. Louis; Becker thrived on the status quo. The closest Becker came to raising ire in the community was in his lack of support for introducing the merit system to City Hall. Adopting a merit system for city employees meant kicking out many of his cronies, and that Becker was not eager to do. Becker gave himself wholeheartedly to the war effort and enthusaistically posed for photographs in his civil defense hat and armband or with an ornamental cannon being prepared for the scrap drive.

Far more important to both St. Louis and the war effort than Becker was Thomas N. Dysart, president of the St. Louis Chamber of Commerce. At sixty-two Dysart had been active in the city's mercantile life for years as an investment banker. During World War I he directed the Liberty Loan drive for the Eighth Federal Reserve District, and in 1924 was chairman of the Community Fund. In 1927 Dysart was one of the backers of Charles A. Lindbergh's flight to Paris and one of the reason's Lindbergh named his plane *The Spirit of St. Louis*. He became vice president of the Chamber of Commerce in 1925 and president in 1934 during the grim days of the depression. Even then, when it seemed that the sun would not shine again, Dysart was known as "a man of friendliness and good humor, of boundless enthusiasm and great abilities."

After the declaration of war, Dysart made the Chamber into a "war agency" which supported every defense effort that touched the city, from Bundles for Britain to victory gardens. Dysart himself chaired the city's first million-dollar bond drive. In the spring of 1943 Dysart became convinced that the war would end soon and that St. Louis ought to start preparing for peace. He helped to organize a postwar planning committee to pave the way to reconversion to peacetime production and to smooth the upheaval that was bound to come with the return of 150,000 servicemen to the city.

On August 1, a warm Sunday afternoon, Becker and Dysart met at Lambert Field, greeting each other with jokes about the adventure ahead of them. The two old friends had agreed to demonstrate their support for the air industry in St. Louis to a crowd of 5,000, by taking a ride in a new Robertson Aircraft glider. Maj. William B. Robertson,

Globe-Democrat *photographer Jack Zehrt shot the horrifying plunge of the glider carrying the mayor of St. Louis, the president of the Chamber of Commerce, and several other officials to their deaths.*

president of the company and head of the Missouri National Guard, was to accompany them in the CG-4A glider, along with Max H. Doyne, director of utilities in St. Louis; Charles L. Cunningham, deputy comptroller; Judge Henry L. Mueller; Harold A. Krueger; and the pilot, Lt. Col. Paul H. Hazelton.

The planes took off without incident. The glider, while still attached to the lead plane, made a pass around the field, then flew out of sight for a few moments. As it came back into view, the cable between the two planes was disconnected. Seconds later the right wing of the glider buckled and fell off. Then, even before

The new St. Louis mayor, Aloys P. Kaufmann, and his wife.

spectators could react, the plane itself plunged 2,000 feet to the center of the field. The wife of Charles L. Cunningham watched. "The glider just crumbled in the sky," she said later, "like a toy falling to pieces. I watched and couldn't believe it, like a horrible nightmare when you know you're dreaming but can't wake up."

All those aboard the glider were killed instantly. Debris from the wreck was scattered around the field, and emergency crews ran to cover the gruesome scene. "There wasn't a sound," said one of the first men to reach the wreck, "not even a moan." The crowd, too, was quiet, stunned as it packed up and went home, leaving officials to sift through the pieces and ask, what went wrong?

The army immediately ordered a full inquiry, which began early the next morning. At first the collapse of a wing strut seemed the most likely explanation, but a few days later a defective wing fitting was found and blamed — it had been milled until it was much too narrow for the slot. (In fact, it was one-twelfth the size it should have been.) But the Army Air Corps still was not satisfied and sent its top investigators to St. Louis to uncover the whole story. A federal grand jury was called.

In December the grand jury's report was made public. It accused Robertson Aircraft Company, which assembled the glider, and its inspectors of dereliction of duty, and it charged Gardner Metal Products Company, the subcontractor, with being "careless and shirking its moral responsibility," because it had not inspected the wing strut fittings. It also denounced the War Department for failing to require inspections of all gliders. But there were no federal statutes on which to base indictments, so nothing more could be done. Shortly before the war ended, Robertson Aircraft went out of business. And gliders proved to be so unsafe that the army discontinued their use after the invasion.

Within hours after Becker's death, Aloys P. Kaufmann, attorney and president of the board of aldermen, was sworn in as the new mayor. Kaufmann was newly-married and he and his bride, like so many other St. Louisans, were searching almost desperately for a place to live.

Housing in St. Louis during the war, as in every American city, was no joke, but apartment seekers tried to keep a sense of humor as they searched for a place to live. Families with small children had an especially difficult time. Willaim Scheid, an inspector at Laister-Kauffmann Aircraft Company, spent some time composing an ad for "Wanted to Rent" after being rebuffed by some 200 landlords because of his four children, who were aged two to six.

> Children, they say, are heaven sent,
>> But to have them means you cannot rent.
> I've done my best, as has my spouse,
>> But to save our soul, we can't find a house.
> Landlords, it seems, were born full grown,
>> Or so you'd think to hear them moan,
> But surely somewhere there must be a few
>> Who also love little children too.
> If one of you should see this ad,
>> Rent us your house, and you won't be sad.
> We'll be good tenants as you will see,
>> If you call DElmar 0903.

(He hadn't a nibble after a week.)

Some families, particularly ones where the husband and father was gone, experimented with living arrangements that allowed two families to share the same dwelling. In a typical household, one mother worked the night shift and the other the day shift and in that way were able to provide full-time care for the children. The John Nooter Boiler Works was especially sensitive to the housing needs of its employees and bought up every nearby house offered for sale.

St. Louisans in the armed forces who wrote home or visited on leave gave a vivid picture of what the war was like. Commander (later Admiral) Charles L. LaBarge stated flatly that the battle for Guadalcanal was "a nightmare," the worst thing he'd ever lived through. But Lt. (jg) Morton D. May, son of the president of the May Company, who arrived on Guadalcanal after the battle, descibed life on the island as

A row of Army Air Corps aviation cadets stands inspection before their biplanes at Parks Air College (now Parks College of Saint Louis University), sometime during World War II.

similar to a camping trip, "a Boy Scout's life."

"The food was naturally bad," he said, "but when I was a Boy Scout the food I cooked wasn't so good either."

A Washington University student, Ensign Philip M. Joyce, became the youngest U.S. officer ever assigned to the Asiatic fleet. He was killed in the Pacific at the age of twenty-one. To honor him, a destroyer was given his name.

Col. James Doolittle, long a favorite with St. Louisans, was made a St. Louis Rotarian for life after his dramatic Tokyo raid. In his acceptance speech, Doolittle noted that he had spent ten happy years in St. Louis (with the Shell Oil Company) and was delighted with the honor.

The Third Bond Drive, chaired by Walter H. Head, began in September. This one was christened "Back the Attack" drive, because at last it seemed that the Allies were on the offensive in both theaters of war. McDonnell Aircraft employees were the first to exceed their quota of bonds, and Ralston Purina had the highest per-capita bond purchases, which entitled them to receive the Butch O'Hare trophy.

For the first time, city-wide response to the drive was sluggish. A Hollywood Cavalcade of Stars visited the city to drum up support, but even Dick Powell, Lucille Ball, Jose Iturbi, Betty Hutton, Harpo Marx, James Cagney, and Judy Garland couldn't move St. Louisans. By the eighth day of the campaign, only thirty-two percent of the goal had been reached. A week later fifty percent had been realized. St. Louis was far behind the rest of the nation. Ads for bonds stepped up their emotional appeal ("GIs give their lives; you lend your money") and at last, after a week's extension, the goal of $180,675,000 was

Maj. Lansing E. Ray, Jr., son of the publisher of the *Globe Democrat,* described his ordeal aboard a torpedoed ship on its way to North Africa early in 1943:

Two thirty a.m., unbelievable explosion woke us out of sound sleep — knew exactly what had happened, couldn't have been anything else — glass shattered all over furniture and everything else loose in the cabin upside down all over the place. Heavy list within 15 seconds — lights out — all six jumped up and dressed hurriedly in shambles, everyone in everyone else's way — feeling of bewilderment mixed with terror — my clothes had all been laid out right next to me, flashlight at my head within easy reach, but one of the others had taken my life belt and it seemed an interminable time before I found another. Grabbed musette bag already packed with emergency items . . . and tin hat. To boat stations . . . — everyone orderly as far as we could see.

". . . sat huddled in the dark on deck — brillant moon, could see life boats with nurses pulling away, and destroyers that had not gone on circling around searching for sub and dropping depth charges — convoy had gone on. [After several hours, Ray was still waiting to be evacuated.]

Suddenly a great muffled explosion, sounding like a huge thud, and 100 feet of thick flame shot out of the funnel right above me — intense heat — men at gun positions clambered down and I was off top deck like a flash. Flames followed by mixture of flame and black smoke, very dense — learned later that engine room had been on fire since half an hour after we were hit and finally boilers had exploded — that was why the destroyers were hurrying to get everyone off ship. . . .

Officer up from below says that heat is intense and paint peeling off walls — would the damn thing blow to bits with us still on it? Finally we were herded slowly aft along the starboard side toward destroyer — threw bag and helmet onto deck of destroyer and slid down greasy cable after them — off that burning ship at last, thank God!

reached.

The metropolitan St. Louis bond drive chairman, Meredith C. Jones, said of the struggle to reach the goal, "The battle of St. Louis was won by fighters of all ranks. This was no easy victory. Our government asked us to back the attack. . . . That we succeeded is the measure of the determination of every one of us that our sector of the

Mr. and Mrs. Louis Nolfo, Italian immigants who were designated "enemy aliens," in the window of their home beneath a flag with five stars for their five sons in the military.

Courtesy Nolfo family

financial beachhead would be held, even as men from St. Louis at the same time held their beachheads at Salerno and on New Guinea.''

The Cardinals lost a lot of players during the year as the draft and enlistments took their toll. At one point the team was so depleted that it advertised in the *Sporting Times* for ''experienced ballplayers.''

Cardinal captain Terry Moore was one of those who left. He wrote a farewell letter to the people of St. Louis shortly before he joined his unit. ''I can't describe with words my appreciation for the way I've been treated in the home town,'' he said. ''You've been wonderful to me. I was responsible for defeats by our club in many, many games — striking out, or failing to get a hit that would drive in a winning run.

''I do not recall one instance when I've been jeered out at Sports-man's Park. I didn't catch every fly that was hit onto center field, either. I can tell you that I was inspired with that wonderful treatment in my first season with the Cards in 1935. Good-by to everyone in baseball, to everyone in St. Louis.''

Despite such losses, the Cardinals won the National League pennant again in 1943 and again came up against the New York Yankees in the World Series. But this time the Yankees won the championship.

One-time presidential candidate Wendell Willkie was a frequent and popular visitor to St. Louis, often as a fund-raiser for the Red Cross or war bonds. In October he came to St. Louis to address a meeting of Republicans. He was met by an annoyed Edgar M. Queeny, president of Monsanto Chemical Company. Queeny had been a major backer in Willkie's 1940 presidential race, but had quickly become disenchanted with the man.

The five Nolfo sons: (from left) Staff Sgt. Ralph, Staff Sgt. Leo, Corp. Louis, Tech. Sgt. Frank, and Pvt. Joseph.

At a meeting between the two men, where Monsanto secretaries took down every word, Willkie said to Queeny, "I don't know whether you're going to support me or not, and I don't give a damn. You're a bunch of political liabilities anyway." Queeny saw Willkie's leaning toward New Deal philosophy as the real liability. "Our free enterprise system," said Queeny, "should be made completely competitive, irrespective of whose toes are trampled upon. This is real liberalism."

In mid-October the coal miners struck again. This time the results were more serious. Thirteen thousand homes in the St. Louis area were said to be without coal and unlikely to get any because defense plants had the first priority. By early November 1,600 miners had closed the Belleville pits.

Under the direction of Smoke Commissioner Raymond R. Tucker, St. Louis had adopted a stiff ordinance that required the burning of hard (anthracite) coal which came only from the East. Burning soft Illinois coal had led to countless smoke palls which caused serious damage to buildings and lungs. Because of the coal strike and subsequent shortage, Secretary of the Interior Ickes ordered St. Louis to go back to using soft coal. But there was a shortage of that kind, too.

On November 1 Missouri Pacific Railroad announced that it had a thirteen-day supply of coal and it would give first priority to shipments of war materials and last priority to civilian passenger trains. The utili-

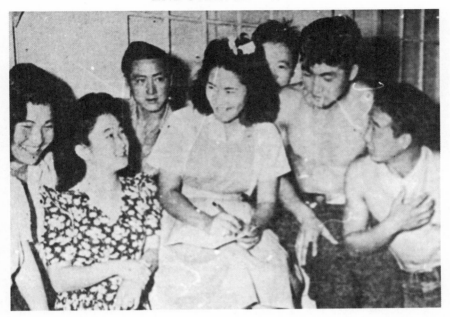

*After three years of war, Nisei (American-born Japanese) were gradually al-
lowed to return to American society. A large community of them farmed the area
west of Chesterfield.*

ty companies (which supplied defense plants as well as households) had
a six- to ten-day supply. The Coal Exchange announced that it could
fill no more orders for householders, not even for those whose bins were
empty. It had been a mild fall, but on November 8, the temperature
fell below freezing and snow flurries announced the beginning of
winter. Homeowners bought wood and gas stoves and bundled up.
Roosevelt told the nation: The coal must be mined; it will be mined.
Eventually it was.

The delivery of both coal and fuel oil was "spasmodic" in
December. Coal allocation centers were established where coal was
meted out to the desperate, and fuel oil users were allowed one
emergency allocation if their supplies were exhausted and they were in
danger of freezing. An flu epidemic in mid-December added to the
misery, but health officials said there was "no cause for alarm." There
would not be a repeat of the disastrous 1918 influenza epidemic.

As the federal government began to relax its policy on the intern-
ment of nisei the War Relocation Authority sent about 150 to the St.
Louis area. They were agricultural workers, professionals, students,
and domestic workers. Phi Beta Kappa Setsuko Matsunaga, who
enrolled in Washington University's graduate school, said, "When
people ask me am I Japanese, I always tell them I am an American of

The Rohwer Relocation Camp for Japanese-Americans was at McGehee, Arkansas. Many were sent from this camp to the St. Louis area.

Japanese descent." Her master's thesis was a sociological analysis of the experiences of Japanese-Americans who had been uprooted and transplanted to St. Louis. She concluded that true democracy is the acceptance of diversity and that differences must be tolerated. A group of Japanese-Americans who had been relocated from the West Coast to the truck farms near Gumbo made a forty dollar contribution to the War Chest campaign in 1943.

In October the number of gasoline coupons drivers were allowed was cut. Holders of A books were allowed only three gallons a week instead of four, and B and C book holders had to prove they were sharing rides before their applications for renewals were accepted. In order to conserve both gasoline and rubber tires, hundreds of stop signs were removed from intersections and a 35 mph speed limit was enforced, which caused more grumbling than any other imposition. Many bus stops, too, were eliminated.

The rubber shortage peaked in November. The critical period would last until spring, said the government, when it was hoped that the production of synthetic rubber would catch up with the demand. Only necessary driving was allowed. Anyone caught pleasure driving lost future rationing coupons — and was fined as well.

Just before Thanksgiving ordnance production slowed. Ten thousand workers were laid off at U.S. Cartridge between Thanksgiving and the first of the year. McQuay-Norris, too, slowed its production and began giving workers time off, beginning with a four-day Thanksgiving holiday.

The layoff at the ordnance plant did not mean a corresponding slowdown in the city's economy. Twelve thousand jobs in the area were still unfilled, and four to five thousand were needed at once for the manufacture of electrical equipment and paper boxes, in the food industry and in the public utilities. Another two thousand workers were sought for non-manufacturing jobs.

In December, when the fortunes of war had turned at last in favor of the Allies, the Office of Civil Defense decided to shift its emphasis to war services, especially to the recovery of salvage, the support of war bonds drives, and the cultivation of victory gardens.

On December 10 news reached St. Louis that Lt. Edward H. O'Hare had been lost November

Courtesy Faye Elliss

Faye Elliss, right, and other USO volunteers decorated this Christmas tree at Union Station.

27 in mid-Pacific while fighting a force of thirty to forty Japanese planes, which were attacking a U.S. aircraft carrier. O'Hare was the leader of a group of F6F Hellcats, navy fighter planes. His daughter Kathleen had been born at DePaul Hospital only nine months earlier. The city — and the nation — mourned the loss of one of their finest sons.

As St. Louis prepared for another wartime Christmas, its defenders were not forgotten. Junior Red Cross volunteers from Blewett and Rosati-Kain high schools made 140,000 articles for GIs — a national record. The presents included afghans, lap robes, and stuffed animals. They also turned out 3,000 stockings, 2,000 greeting cards, 400 tray favors, 500 ice cream decorations, and 6,100 menu covers for Scott Field, Jefferson Barracks, and Fort Leonard Wood. In their spare time they put together 1,000 Christmas packages for children who had been evacuated from occupied countries.

Merchants reported that yule sales were at an all-time high as shoppers opened their "wartime purses." The sale of luxury items had doubled from the previous year — jewelry, perfume and furs were the favorite gifts. Arthur B. Baer, president of Stix Baer and Fuller, said "This year the Christmas rush started in October and continued till Christmas Eve."

In the midst of the gaiety President Roosevelt delivered a somber

Christmas message to Americans. ''We still have much to face in the way of further suffering and sacrifice and personal tragedy,'' he said. He stressed that peace will come, ''though the cost may be high and the time may be long. . . . There is no easy road to victory and the end is not yet in sight.''

Three days after Christmas a rail strike threatened and Roosevelt did not wait to see if it would materialize. Invoking the Smith-Conally Act, he took over the railroads; 25,000 railroad employees in St. Louis suddenly found themselves working for the federal government. The nineteen trunk lines, four short lines, and five switching lines in the area were put under the direction of Maj. William A. W. Von Gehr, the army district transportation officer. But within twenty-four hours, the railway unions canceled the planned strike and travel went on as usual.

Days later, a subdued St. Louis celebrated New Year's Eve with a fraction of the liquor that it had enjoyed before — even beer was scarce. Roosevelt had designated January 1 as a national day of prayer. On New Year's Day, St. Louisans soberly took stock of the nation's victories and losses — and prayed.

THE THIRD YEAR — 1944
INVASION

THE WHOLE WORLD — including the Germans — knew that 1944 was the year for an attempted Allied invasion of Europe. But no one — not even Supreme Allied Commander Gen. Dwight D. Eisenhower — knew when and where it would happen. Planning the logistics and armaments for the invasion had begun in 1943. To ready the troops, defense plants stepped up production for the first three months of 1944. Night and day, airplanes, landing craft, and tanks rolled off assembly lines all over the nation, and ammunition poured from ordnance plants.

St. Louis contributed heavily to the pre-invasion buildup. As many as eighty-eight local firms were producing materiel for army and navy landing craft in 1944, primarily for LSTs (Landing Ship, Tank), LCTs (Landing Craft, Tank), LVTs (Landing Vehicle, Tracked) and the amphibious DUKWs (D = designed in 1942, U = utility, K = front wheel drive, W = two rear driving axles). In January alone, $12 million worth of equipment was ordered by the government from St. Louis firms.

The largest area contractor for the navy was St. Louis Shipbuilding and Steel Co., which built LST's. It was followed by Stupp Bros. Bridge and Iron Co. and Mississippi Valley Structural Steel, which together turned out LCTs from their shared shipyard in Quincy, Illinois. Midwest Piping & Supply made fittings for both LSTs and LSMs (Landing Ship, Medium); Sterling Steel Castings Co. produced parts for various landing craft; Duke Manufacturing outfitted the galleys for LSTs; and Foster Bros. Manufacturers made berths and fittings for LSTs.

Amphibious vehicles also came from St. Louis. When General

St. Louis Car Collection, Washington University Archives

Proud St. Louis Car Company employees pose by the amphibious Water Buffalo assembly line.

George Patton's 7th Army slogged its way to Rome in January 1944, it was accompanied by enormous clumsy "ducks" that bounced along beside it. These amphibious trucks were the army's workhorses. They carted everything from heavy artillery to mess units over countryside so rugged that mules bogged down in it. And they could swim.

Assembled at the St. Louis Chevy plant, the DUKW was thought at first to be the most important new vehicle to be produced since the tank. It had a two-and-a-half ton truck chassis, was thirty-six feet long and eight feet wide, accommodating fifty men or an equivalent load of supplies. On land it had six driving wheels and conventional steering gear; in the water it used a marine propeller and rudder. An ingenious design allowed the driver to shift controls for both wheel and propeller drive, so that it could maneuver in any terrain. Eisenhower called the DUKW's "invaluable."

DUKW's had originally been sent to the South Pacific, but had been used there solely for transportation rather than as assault vehicles. Their first tour of duty as invasion craft came in 1943 in the Sicily campaign. By the time they were sent to Normandy DUKW's had been equipped with deflatable tires. By reducing pressure, they could travel easily on sand. On D day, loaded with 105mm howitzers, numerous DUKW's battled their way onto Omaha Beach.

Other amphibious vehicles were made at the St. Louis Car Com-

Courtesy Mrs. W. Thornhill

A St. Louis-built LST docked near the Eads Bridge and brought a crowd to the downtown levee.

St. Louis Car Collection,
Washington University Archives

The Water Buffalo was tested during trial runs in Spanish Lake.

A trainman waves DUKWs through the St. Louis railyards. Two hundred such trains left daily.

The Aeronautical Chart plant produced tons of charts for the Air Force. The campaign in the Philippines alone required 714,000 copies of that area.

Tanks at the beginning of the war were extremely primitive. Models posed in this early prototype. It was used at Fort Leonard Wood for practice.

pany, headed by the indefatigable civic leader Edwin Meissner. The firm had made streetcars and buses until the beginning of the war, when it switched over to defense production. In 1942 the first, experimental "Water Buffalo," a naval assault vehicle (LVT-A) appeared. Early models were made of steel without armor plate.

Because Meissner could not get permission to construct new facilities for his factory, he bought some of the old Curtiss-Wright buildings at Lambert Field, had them dismantled, put on railroad cars, and brought to his plant. The procedure was expensive, but it was the only way Meissner could get the necessary space in which to expand.

MAT Hellcat tank destroyers, made in part by Kelvinator of St. Louis, leave an area railyard for Europe.

St. Louis Car Company and American Car and Foundry Company of St. Charles both produced tanks which headed for Berlin. In the summer of 1940 the United States had a total of sixty-four tanks. Immediately after Pearl Harbor the army sent out an anguished call for 7,635 more at once. A crash production program was started, for tanks and for all other army vehicles. Automobile, truck, bus, streetcar, railway car, and locomotive manufacturers began to fill orders for the military. Tanks made up an important part of their output.

American tanks were heavily criticized almost before they came off the assembly line. The German Panther and Tiger (as well as the Russian tanks) were far superior to anything used by Americans. But the War Department could see that tanks would be as important to the Second Front as aircraft were to the Pacific theater, and they pressured engineers to come up with an effective design.

After limited use in World War I, tanks were still considered a new weapon in 1941-42. Their manufacture was complicated and expensive. The first tank order of the war, which was given to American Car and Foundry, called for 329 light tanks (M2A4's), each weighing twelve tons and each requiring 2,800 different kinds of parts — 14,000 individual pieces — exclusive of the engine. The engine was an aircraft type, since automotive engines were not large enough to pull such

Post-Dispatch war correspondent Virginia Irwin interviewed a St. Louis glider pilot (and former Saint Louis University student) Joseph Thompson, Jr., who participated in the Normandy invasion.

"We took off with a heavy machine gun to deliver to a certain spot," he told me with a sparkle in his eye. "We ran into fire from some enemy 88s coming down and found that the field was not only too small but neatly fitted with a few posts thoughtfully put there by Germans. Well, when we crashed, there was nothing to do but run for cover."

After lying low for awhile Thompson and his men decided they might as well try to get their ammunition out of the glider and set up a position as die of either boredom or pneumonia lying in a ditch half filled with water. "The attempt was noble but shortlived," Thompson laughingly said. "The enemy opened up with machine guns the minute we moved. If it hadn't been that they drew fire from some 105-millimeter guns on our left flank we probably would all be pushing up a few French daisies by now." Except for further annoyance by German snipers along the way Thompson and his men finally worked their way to a command post, received instructions on how to find their way back to the beach and arrived there about 2 in the morning only to find that jerries were strafing the beach. . . .

Finally, after hours of waiting, Thompson and his men were taken off the beach on a duck . . . and taken out to an LCI.

"If the Jerries hadn't decided to dive bomb that LCI after everything else we went through I might be less anxious to get back, but dive bombing that LCI was the last straw," Thompson continued. He gave a vicious chomp to some gum he was chewing.

weight. (Later, two Cadillac engines were used.) ACF had to make its own face-hardened plate for armor. The alternative was to use a patchwork of armor pieces riveted to the outside, which was highly unsatisfactory.

During the entire course of the war, tank production was hampered by a steady stream of engineering changes and by difficulties with armor plating. General Steel Castings Corporation of Granite City, Illinois, and Eddystone, Pennsylvania, designed and produced the first one-piece armor hull, which rapidly became the standard for all tanks. In fact, the tonnage of steel castings in the St. Louis area was reputed to be more than twice the combined tonnage of any other two casting

Many St. Louis firms supplied parts for antiaircraft guns for the armed forces.

centers. American Steel Foundries of Granite City was one of the many area foundries which supplied steel for the operation.

American Car and Foundry, in both its St. Charles and Berwick, Pennsylvania, plants, produced the greatest number of tanks for the army — 15,224, or 17.2 percent of the total. As the tank evolved from the M3 (Grant) to the M4 (Sherman) to the M5, ACF kept pace with the changes, often interrupting production for retooling.

Another important component of the invasion force was the glider. Gliders, since they did not require engines and expensive navigation equipment and since they usually contained more wood than metal, could be produced much faster and cheaper than airplanes. Three St. Louis companies made gliders — St. Louis Aircraft Company (a subsidiary of St. Louis Car), Robertson Aircraft, and Laister-Kauffmann. Kilgen Organ Company turned from their specialty — they had worked on the magnificent organs at St. Patrick's Cathedral and at Carnegie Hall in New York City — and molded plastic plywood into glider subassemblies for Robertson. Anheuser-Busch also acted as a subcontractor for Robertson, and Koken Companies made wings for Laister-Kauffmann gliders, which were assembled at the Arena. Export Packing Company and Wiles-Chipman Lumber Company made crates for shipping gliders to combat zones.

St. Louis Aircraft experimented with high-capacity gliders, specifically with the XCG-111, a huge, cargo-carrying vehicle intended

to take part i   ıt abruptly
plans were   . Laister-
Kauffmann t   Horse,'' a
glider that cc   their supplies, or ever   the glider
could be broı   nding. Its
nose wheel re   ;pace.

 Robertson   ⁷en before
the tragic cra: ɔd several
prominent St   nspection
because of det   andard in
one inspectior   roduction
in March.

 Neither the   apanese-
held islands in   ıe use of
bombs. Durinɡ   _____ ᴜᴜ,ᴜᴜᴜ,ᴜᴜ0 bombs
of seventy different types and sizes. A typical bomb consisted of a body
or casing, fins, explosive and fuse. (Primers, boosters, and adapters
could be added, but were not necessary.) The completed bomb,
assembled and loaded, was the end product of a series of manufacturing operations which involved several different plants. All components
except the explosive were usually provided by private industry.
Government ordnance plants produced the explosives.

 Bomb production began early in 1942 and peaked in the fall of 1944.
(In 1940 there were only six manufacturers of explosives in the entire
nation.) American bombs ranged from the four-pound "butterflies,"
which were usually dropped in clusters, to the 22,000-pound "grand
slam" bombs, which were used in the saturation bombing of Germany
and Japan in 1944-45. Half of all the bombs produced in the United
States were medium bombs of 500 pounds, and most of them came
from the St. Louis Ordnance District.

 Before Pearl Harbor, bombs for Lend-Lease were made by machin-
ing down a solid steel billet, gouging out the interior and filling it with
TNT or amatol. After the war began, it became obvious that this procedure was much too slow. Someone devised the method of using a
short length of thick-walled, large-diameter pipe. One end was brought
to white heat in a furnace and hammered into a "tail"; the other end
became the "nose." The case was sandblasted to remove the scale,
heat-treated to harden the steel, cut and threaded to receive the fuse,
finned, painted, inspected and sent to a government ordnance plant.
There it was filled with explosives and the fuse was installed. It was
armed as close to the intended target as possible.

 St. Louis was already a center for pipe production, and stove companies like Empire Stove, American Stove and Wrought Iron Range

seemed to be especially adaptable to bomb production. Midwest Piping & Supply produced tons of 1,000-pound demolition bomb casings, and Scullin Steel turned out the giant "earthquake" bombs (12,000 pounds) for the RAF. U.S. forces rarely used bombs weighing over 10,000 pounds before 1945, but the giants were well-suited to the British bombers Lancaster and Halifax.

St. Louis manufacturers also built practice bombs, chemical bombs, aircraft flares, fragmentation bombs, anti-tank mines and depth charges. Bomb casings made in the area were usually filled with TNT or DNT at the Weldon Spring Ordnance Works operated by the Atlas Powder Company. In the spring of 1944,

A workman checks tolerances on a locally-produced blockbuster bomb.

when it looked as if enough bombs had been stockpiled to win the war, the Weldon Spring facility shut down, laying off thousands of workers, only to reopen six months later for the desperate final push during the winter of 1944-45.

In April 1944 several employees of the ordnance works charged their employer with squandering manpower and destroying vital war materials. Affidavits related stories of gambling and idleness at the plant, of mushroom-picking and swimming pool scrubbing on company time by employees who should have been producing bombs. Upon investigation, the charges evaporated and even the waste-watchdog, Sen. Harry S. Truman, refused to bring his investigative committee to St. Louis to follow up on the story.

Building a fuse was the most delicate step of bomb production. A fuse had to have the precision of a fine watch, yet be able to withstand the violent shock of impact. The greatest producer of bomb fuses in the St. Louis Ordnance District was a hairpin manufacturer in southern Illinois who converted an old livery stable into the nation's outstanding arming wire shop. Carter Carburetor of St. Louis also made bomb fuses. Most of the other fuses made in the area, however, were for the artillery, rather than for aerial bombs.

Shipping tons of bombs to a destination hundreds or thousands of

The Fisher Body plant at Union and Natural Bridge made 105-mm howitzers.

miles away required extreme care in packaging. Alton Boxboard Company came up with an award-winning idea for wrapping 10,000-pound bombs and, coincidentally, took the lion's share of the area's scrap paper to do so. Gaylord Container Corporation and Paper Convertors also made packing rings for bombs.

At Midwest Piping & Supply bombs were "autographed" with a stylus by those who paid for the privilege by buying bonds. In July Lt. C. Stacy Weaks wrote to his mother in St. Louis from his Liberator Squadron in England that for each $1000 bond purchased, he would personally drop an autographed bomb on an enemy target and record where and when it was dropped for the purchaser.

Although St. Louis was not a great center for artillery production, several key components were manufactured here. Jackes-Evans developed and produced disintegrating links for machine gun cartridges, which freed that weapon for use by rapidly-advancing troops. S. G. Adams made machine gun mounts; Johnston Tin Foil & Metal Co. received an "E" for producing parts for navy ack-ack guns; Knapp-Monarch turned out grenade launchers and VT (proximity) fuses; Measuregraph Co. made mortar shells and parts; and Mines Equipment Co. manufactured parts for the 155mm "Long Toms."

Several months before D day Lt. Col. James H. Howard of St. Louis, as leader of a squadron of P-51 aircraft, was providing support for a heavy bomber mission on the continent when a number of Nazi fighters attacked the group. Col. Howard engaged the enemy, downing

The German battleship Tirpitz *was sunk in Norway's Tromso Fjord by an earthquake bomb made at Scullin Steel.*

Courtesy Delores Bertels

Workers at Weldon Spring Ordnance Works packaged TNT. Many of the jobs there were classified top secret.

an ME 110. Abruptly he lost contact with his group and returned to the bombers. Seeing that they were being attacked with no support, he singlehandedly attacked the formation of thirty German airplanes. For thirty minutes he fought them off, destroying three and damaging more. Three of his guns went out of action and his fuel supply became dangerously low. Nonetheless, he continued to attempt to protect the bombers until he was forced to turn back. For his "skill, courage and intrepidity," Col. Howard (a shy man who told reporters, shucks, he didn't do anything special) was award the Medal of Honor on June 5, 1944.

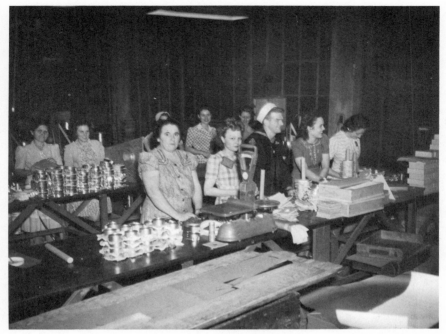

Courtesy Dolores Will

The assembly line at Johnston Tin Foil turned out foil used to scramble enemy radar.

That same day, at 11:37 P.M., St. Louis radio stations picked up a flash from a German news agency that the Allied invasion of Europe had begun. Thirty minutes later, shortly after midnight on June 6, the information was confirmed by Allied sources: ''This is D day.'' At last the tension of waiting was broken. In St. Louis thousands spent the day in prayer. A hastily-called interfaith service was held at the Soldiers' Memorial, and schools held patriotic assemblies to commemorate the event.

After D day the Allies optimistically predicted the war would end ''any day.'' Some two dozen St. Louis defense contractors were released from their contracts and told they could begin producing civilian goods again. War Production Board chief Donald Nelson said it was time for an ''orderly reconversion.'' Layoffs began at the major war plants. At first it was predicted that as many as 12,500 workers would lose their jobs; a few months later the figure was revised to 28,000. Other defense workers, feeling the insecurity in the air, began looking for more permanent jobs. And nervous union members throughout the area began walking out on strike with monotonous regularity. They wanted assurance that the widespread unemployment of the depression would not return, but such assurance could not be given.

In an attempt to control postwar economic development, the Chamber of Commerce had begun preparing a peacetime plan for the city in 1943. Working with Mayor Kaufmann, the Chamber came up with an ambitious proposal which involved the construction of new highways, housing and office buildings. Jobs for 710,000 people — almost 100,000 more than were then in the labor force — were expected to be available.

But in the spring of 1944, those hopes were far from a reality. Hundreds of veterans were returning to St. Louis and expecting to find either their old job waiting or a better one. Morton J. May, president of Famous Barr Co., guaranteed his former employees in the service that their old jobs would be offered to them "regardless of their physical condition," in compliance with the Selective Service Act. But not all employers were so ready to comply, and workers themselves were not eager to give up a job for a returning vet. At a public discussion of the problem held at Kiel Auditorium, one speaker warned, "Competition between returning vets and civilian workers for jobs in the postwar era may lead to civil war, if there are not jobs for all."

Readjusting to civilian life was difficult enough for the able-bodied servicemen who returned. For those who had been disabled, the chore was especially tough. About 650 disabled vets entered the St. Louis job market each month in 1944. A "Jobs for Heroes" program on radio station KXOK helped find them work and so did the Chamber of Commerce's special bureau for veteran employment. A new category of disabled was made for those suffering from "battle fatigue," a profound depression that came with seeing too much horror, grief, and pain.

Of course many St. Louisans were not coming back at all. By mid-1944, 522 St. Louisans in the service had been killed in battle, 159 had lost their lives in the line of duty other than on the battlefield, and 67 had died of disease. Although the numbers were heart-breaking, it was ironic to note that more St. Louisans had been killed at home in accidents (964) since Pearl Harbor, than had died in the war. In fact, across the nation, the same was true — industrial accidents alone killed 5,000 more Americans than combat did, and the injury-disabled equaled sixty times the number of combat-disabled.

But the sorrow of the families of the war dead was not mitigated by such statistics. Mayor Kaufmann wrote a personal letter to each bereaved family and tried to express the sympathy of the city. His message ended, "I firmly believe that the history of this great nation is written in the toil, the sacrifice and even in the death of those who have fought for the principles for which it stands. The nation's foundation is the graves of its heroes."

News of the invasion of Normandy was greeted with jubilation and hope.

By the end of July it became apparent that the Axis powers were far from defeated, that the war would continue at least through the winter, and that production of defense materiel was lagging badly. General Eisenhower cabled from the field that troops were using four times as much ammunition as expected and supplies were running dangerously low. At St. Lo alone, fifteen hours of sustained fire had depleted reserves.

St. Louis industry again turned to full defense production. During the fall the need for new workers climbed from 10,000 to 22,700. Radio and newspaper ads exhorted workers to return to the war plants for the duration, but St. Louisans were slow to respond.

St. Louisans were also slow to respond to other calls to patriotism during 1944, much slower than they had been in 1943 or 1942. All the scrap drives faltered and only the enthusiasm of school children kept the paper drive alive.

Increasingly emotional appeals were made to homemakers to save and recycle fat. One ad showed a young wounded GI calling to his mother for help, "Motherr-r-r!" A pound of grease could be translated into 150 machine gun bullets, four ack-ack shells, two anti-tank shells, or 2,190 smallpox vaccines. Glycerine in the grease was also used to make sulfa drugs and opiates.

Three bond drives were held in 1944 — the fourth, fifth, and sixth of the war. The Fourth War Loan Drive began January 17 with a new approach. Hundreds of Boy Scouts fanned out throughout the area in a

A Red Cross parade on Washington Avenue stirred up support for the blood bank.

door-to-door search for pledges. An all-blind troop set out in pairs with some trepidation but full dedication. Leaflets that the Scouts handed out asked, ''Would you say no to MacArthur or Doolittle?'' and the implication was, then you'd better not say no to us.

Mayor Kaufmann added his exhortation. Only the participation of St. Louisans in bond drives ''has kept our land free of bombs from the sky, free from rubble in your streets, and free from troops of occupation in your living room.'' But even with such rhetoric to chew on, sales of bonds lagged until February 1, when a sudden spurt made that day a record 24-hours in sales.

The reason for the surge was the release of the story of the Bataan death march of 1942. At least 10,000 Allied troops died from disease, hunger, or brutality on that nightmare trip, and as many as 50,000 were still being held captive, probably enduring unspeakable tortures. As the pledges came in, bond drive chairman Walter J. Hein asserted, ''Let Hirohito and Hitler take this as a partial indication of St. Louis' answer to the barbaric indignities committed against American soldiers on Bataan.'' By February 4, St. Louis was once again leading the nation in bond sales, and by February 12 was again ''over the top.''

A bond rally at the Hotel Chase offered a lighter note and an en-

The Fifth War Bond drive generated money for the war effort.

viable prize — kisses from two movie stars. Errol Flynn's smack brought $10,000 from Mrs. James H. Arthur. Not to be outdone, her husband, president of Fanchon and Marco Service Corporation, paid $25,000 for a buss from actress Gene Tierney.

The Fifth Loan Drive, which began in June, was directed by banker Isaac A. Long, who urged St. Louisans to take their money out of safe deposit boxes, mattresses, and sugar bowls to buy war bonds. Ralph Edwards brought his "Truth or Consequences" show to St. Louis to benefit the bond drive. It was wildly successful.

The Sixth War Loan Drive opened Nov. 20 with James P. Hickok as chairman. Its slogan was "Sock 'em in the Sixth," and again St. Louisans responded generously.

An election year, 1944 was a time of political square dancing at home, and Missouri found itself with one caller — Robert E. Hannegan — and one star dancer — Harry S. Truman. In January Hannegan was named National Democratic Party chairman, and from that point he invested his considerable enthusiasm ("zeal," said one commentator) in orchestrating the Democratic National Convention in Chicago and the various races in the November election.

Early in the year, a spoiler entered the picture. Gerald L. K. Smith, one-time Disciples of Christ minister and current director of the America First Party, came to St. Louis to recruit "Defenders of

The Sixth War Loan drive was kicked off with a dramatic nighttime parade.

Christ's Cause," that is, anti-Semitic white supremacists. St. Louis representatives of the Veterans of Foreign Wars, Jewish War Vets, and the American Legion called Smith a "demagogic, unAmerican, Fascist rabble rouser," but that didn't keep him from drawing a healthy crowd to Kiel Auditorium.

On Smith's third visit in March, Oscar A. Earhardt, secretary of the St Louis Industrial Union Council, made a plea to Mayor Kaufmann for a patriotic rally to be held at the same time as Smith's "to make clear that while St. Louis has given the America First party the right to use a city-owned hall, the city is aware of the sinister potentialities of this group and rejects its purpose." However, Smith continued to find St. Louis congenial and made his headquarters here in 1946, promising to "drink the blood of Jews" when he became president of the United States.

The GOP held its convention the last week in June. New York Governor Thomas E. Dewey was nominated on the first ballot; Governor John W. Bricker of Ohio was chosen as his running mate. Dewey had been a popular governor with a reputation for both independence from traditional political strings and rectitude. *Time* said, "Dewey wore no man's collar. (His own choice in collars might seem a bit unfashionably stiff, but the U.S. would get used to that.) Thus unencumbered, he could move with absolute precision, unhampered by due bills, to the tasks ahead."

Two weeks later President Roosevelt agreed to run for a fourth term. "Reluctantly, as a good soldier, I will accept," he said. Obviously he was a tired man; he had aged dramatically since 1941. The choice of a vice presidential running mate, therefore, was especially important. The list of possibilities was long and included House Speaker Sam

Robert E. Hannegan, chairman of the Democratic National Committee in 1944. Later, President Harry Truman appointed him postmaster general.

Rayburn, Senator Alben Barkley, economic adviser Jimmy Byrnes, WMC boss Paul V. McNutt, and "the grey little junior Senator from Missouri," Harry S. Truman.

The 1944 Gridiron show presented by the Women's Advertising Club of St. Louis featured a parody of the popular song "Rosie the Riveter." Called "Rosie [Roosevelt] Is Riveted," it showed how hard it was to get the chief executive out of the White House, despite the hopes of Republican candidates.

> Willkie: Ladies and gents if you vote for me
> I'll make duck soup out of Franklin D.
>
> Chorus: No matter how you shout
> You'll never get him out
> Rosie . . . is riveted!
>
> Dewey: I am the guy to be president
> I have glamour and I'm eloquent.
>
> Chorus: Oh, Dewey, it's no use,
> You'll never get him loose,
> Rosie . . . is riveted!
>
> [Robert] Taft: Rosie's been in here for 12 years,
> Twelve years is long enough —
>
> Chorus: You're talking through your hat,
> This is his habitat,
> Rosie . . . is riveted!

The week of the convention in mid-July, rumors buzzed from one end of the nation to the other, and columnists speculated on "what Harold Ickes said to Sidney Hillman, what the president told Claude Pepper" and who would come out on top in the vice presidential scrimmage. During the convention, Hannegan juggled labor, southern interests, northern industrialists, civil rights leaders, internationalists, and superpatriots, keeping everyone within speaking distance of each other. Then suddenly it was all over and the modest little man from Independence had carried away the prize on the second ballot. Harry Truman, long a familiar figure in St. Louis, was the man who would campaign alongside FDR.

For the first time since Reconstruction, the status of the American Negro became a political issue in 1944. In March, two days before the U.S. Supreme Court ruled that Negroes in Texas had the right to vote in a primary election, the St. Louis Board of Aldermen held a secret session to discuss allowing

Gerald L. K. Smith, head of the America First Party, found a sympathetic audience in St. Louis.

blacks to eat in the lunchroom at City Hall. The *Post-Dispatch* called the measure "too hot" to vote on and predicted that it would die a natural death. Instead, the aldermen passed it resoundingly — twenty-two to four — and thus made it a misdemeanor to refuse service on the basis of race, color, or creed.

But the new ordinance did not apply to private eating places. In May a uniformed black sailor walked into a five-and-ten cent store at the corner of Sixth and Washington. Since the lunch counter was crowded, he stood and waited to be served. He continued to wait as others, who had come after him, were recognized, seated, and served. Finally he caught the waitress' eye. "We can't serve Negroes here," she said. The sailor was dumbfounded. "But I've been in three engagements," he said. She shook her head. He left the store.

Hearing of the incident, the Citizens Civil Rights Committee of St. Louis made a decision: Jim Crow must go. On May 18 Ruth Mattie Wheeler, wife of NAACP president Henry Wheeler, and Thelma McNeal, wife of state senator Theodore McNeal, sat at the lunch counter at Katz drugstore downtown and waited to be served. Within a matter of minutes, they were lifted up by the arms and escorted out of the store. They showed no resistance.

The next day Pearl Maddox, Myrtle Walker, Birdie Beal Anderson, and Henry Wheeler walked into the lunchroom of Stix Baer and Fuller

The number of wildcat strikes in the St. Louis area seriously impeded the war effort and threatened to create a barrier to the invasion of Europe, as this editorial cartoon from the Star-Times *indicates.*

and sat down. They were not served.

The next week, the next month and the next, throughout the summer, small groups of blacks and whites, members of the Citizens Civil Rights Committee persistently sought the opportunity to eat lunch at Famous Barr, Stix Baer and Fuller, and Scruggs-Vandervoort-Barney. They were persistently refused. Everyone was polite.

The embarrassed management tried to reason with them. "Only strife would result!" they were told, if they ate a bacon, lettuce and tomato sandwich in front of whites. St. Louis "wasn't ready" to share a tuna salad or cup of soup with blacks. Whites accompanying blacks were served, but if they offered a bite of food to their companions, the lunchroom was closed. The management insisted that whites could not tolerate the sight of blacks eating.

The Civil Rights Committee considered the issue carefully and distributed handbills which read, "Fellow Americans! An Appeal to Your Conscience, Your Patriotism, Your Sense of Fair Play and Justice." The committee argued that since the store management was citing the reaction of white customers as the reason that blacks could not be served — "a slanderous libel on your Americanism" — whites should tell management that they would survive the sight of blacks eating lunch. "All of our sons, brothers, fathers and husbands are fighting, suffering and dying; Let us practice, together, that democracy for which all of our boys are dying." The response was silence.

On another front racial barriers began to crack. Saint Louis University decided to open its doors to blacks for the fall semester, goaded by

Mayor Al Kaufmann welcomes Capt. Wendell Pruitt back to the city. The twenty-four-year-old Mustang fighter pilot shot down three Nazi planes, destroyed eight planes on the ground, and helped to sink a Nazi destroyer. On Pruitt's left is his mother, Mrs. Melanie C. Pruitt, and on his right is his sister, Mrs. Edith Payne.

the fiery crusader for justice, Rev. Claude Heithaus, S. J. In the spring of 1944 Rev. Heithaus gave a "scathing denunciation of race discrimination" during a Mass. It's a lie, he claimed, that white students will refuse to attend school with blacks, and continued, "Ignorance is the school of race prejudice, and provincialism is its tutor. Its memory is stuffed with lies and its mind is warped by emotionalism. Pride is its book and snobbery its pen. All the hatred and fears, all the cruelties and prejudices of childhood are perpetuated by it. It binds the intellect and it hardens the heart." He asked the students present who supported his views to rise. The entire congregation stood.

Labor unrest in the city was closely tied to racial unrest. Perhaps the majority of strikes in the area — and there were hundreds of strikes in 1944 — involved racial disputes of some sort. Even at the St. Louis Car Company, where president Meissner, who was also chairman of the city Civil Rights Commission, insisted on a policy of racial tolerance, workers walked off the job because they perceived one race was given advantages over another.

In July eight St. Louis manufacturing plants with government contracts were cited as being unfair to Negro labor. Allegedly they refused to hire or promote blacks. The Fair Employment Practices Commission promised hearings before the end of the year.

In August two incidents increased hostility between the races, and fears of riot again inspired city officials to think of solutions to the

Trying to keep their sense of humor, St. Louis workers were crammed into every available means of transportation during the bus strike.

dilemma. In the first, a black man riding a streetcar asked a white man to extinguish a cigarette, as the smoke offended his wife. The white refused — or denied that he was smoking. After an increasingly heated argument, the black began to beat the white. Before the motorman could stop for help, the white man was dead. The next evening four black women were arrested for allegedly striking a white woman, a soldier's wife, and her four-year-old son, for reasons unknown. City officials and the press called for a cautious response, saying that these were isolated events and not indicative of an impending racial war.

Mayor Kaufmann was committed to racial harmony and was determined to prove that commitment to blacks. He declared December 12 "Captain Wendell O. Pruitt Day." Captain Pruitt, a black pilot with the 302nd Mustang Fighter Squadron, shot down three enemy planes, destroyed eight others on the ground, and helped sink an enemy destroyer. A veteran of seventy missions, he held the Distinguished Flying Cross, the Air Medal, and six oak leaf clusters.

Of all the strikes St. Louis had to endure during 1944, the worst was the two-day strike by streetcar and bus operators and maintenance men. Because of a dispute over overtime pay, drivers staged a wildcat walkout the morning of June 1. It resulted in the most serious traffic congestion the city had ever seen — there was a 400 percent increase in

Most bus drivers were as happy as the passengers when the strike was quickly settled.

the number of cars on the road, as over two hundred thousand St. Louisans decided to get to work one way or another. All downtown traffic signals were turned off, and patrolmen directed traffic at each intersection. Nonetheless, traffic jams at such intersections as 12th and Delmar, Market and Spruce, or Grand and Vandeventer lasted for hours.

Service cars enjoyed a boom, charging twenty-five cents for a ride and shoehorning more people than anyone thought possible into their vehicles. Taxis, too, carried the maximum number of passengers. Most people were angry about the tie-up. All defense plants, as well as other businesses and stores, were hurt. For the two days of the strike, defense production was cut twenty-five percent. Taking advantage of the antagonistic mood, the Communist Party of St. Louis distributed mimeographed handbills along downtown streets urging the city to take over streetcar and bus lines. Neither the St. Louis Public Service Company nor the union could long withstand such public displeasure and both sides came to a quick agreement. Within a few days of the strike's settlement, the furor died down.

The U.S S. Missouri, *the greatest of American dreadnaughts, brought a sense of pride to St. Louisans.*

Two other strikes caused the city problems during the year. Teamsters slammed the doors of their truck cabs and stayed off the job for so long that the government took over several truck lines, including three in St. Louis: Brashear Freight Lines, Park Transportation Co., and Todebusch Transfer, Inc. At the end of November and through the middle of December, movie projectionists called it quits and theaters throughout the area were dark.

River traffic on the Mississippi during the war was as heavy as railroad traffic around St. Louis. Barge lines operating on the Mississippi in 1944 made up the largest fleet of towboats and barges in the river's history. Among new equipment ordered by the War Department were twenty-one 2,000-hp towboats, 100 600-hp intercoastal tugboats, 155 oil barges, 115 convertible steel barges, 260 wooden barges, and 55 dry cargo barges. Each new boat was named after a battle of World War II. The first was the *Wake Island.* Ninety-five percent of river traffic during 1944 was directly related to the war effort. Shipments of grain, ore, crude oil, gasoline, and coal moved from the Great Lakes to the Mississippi, from the Missouri to the Mississippi, from the Illinois to the Mississippi and down to New Orleans and the Gulf.

To accommodate the heavy military traffic, a new bridge was built across the river at Jefferson Barracks. When the bridge opened, it signaled the demise of the last ferry in the St. Louis area, the Davis

Street ferry, which operated along the Carondelet riverfront district. The ferry had had eighty-five years of continuous operation, and had handled as many as 1000 cars and 2,500 foot passengers in one day.

One of the best-known ships of the war was the U.S.S. *Missouri,* a dreadnaught of the Iowa class. With an eye to national politics, Navy officials overlooked Missouri Governor Forrest C. Donnell in favor of Senator Harry S. Truman for the launching of the "mightiest battlewagon of them all." To Donnell's dismay, Truman's daughter Margaret was chosen to christen the *Missouri.*

Once at sea, the Missouri's crew found a flaw in its appointments and cabled the St. Louis Chamber of Commerce for help. Could someone in the state for whom the ship was named send them a coffee pot or hot plate for sick bay? Sam Brown, owner of the Bonnie Butter Products Company, was the first to respond. With great pride, he donated both an electric grill and a coffee pot. As crew members later reported, they were well appreciated.

Two familiar St. Louis names appeared on the police blotter in 1944. Thirty-two year old Presley Straub Anheuser was charged with violating the Selective Service Act, i.e., draft evasion, because he claimed that he was a farmer and therefore exempt from the service. His seventy-eight-acre tract near Villa Ridge was the home of thirty-six registered Hereford cattle, but neighbors complained that Anheuser used the place only to give parties. Countering that he was indeed a serious farmer, Anheuser also pointed out that he was also a "pre-Pearl Harbor father," a necessary condition for exemption. Eventually the U.S. District Attorney decided that the evidence against Anheuser was "flimsy" and recommended that he be paroled.

The second case had no clearcut conclusion and in fact was full of questions from the beginning. On July 16 Auguste Chouteau, Jr., was having supper in a southside tavern when he was accosted by the police. They asked to see his draft card. He didn't have it with him. Employed in the tool room of Midwest Piping & Supply, Chouteau was wearing defense overalls and a badge. Nonetheless, he gave the officers the impression of not being patriotic enough and was arrested.

That night, according to his story, he was held for fifteen hours incommunicado, repeatedly interrogated by the police and occasionally beaten, even though the draft card that they sought was resting at his home. After he was released, Chouteau approached reporters. When they investigated the story, they found that the police report of the incident had been withdrawn from the files and heretofore friendly police sources would supply no information. Initially Chouteau brought charges of police brutality against the force, but failed to show up for the hearing and the case was dropped.

Mrs. Albert Kiers and Mrs. Caroline Houwink (right) organized relief efforts for the destitute Dutch.

St. Louisans with ties to Europe alternatively grieved and rejoiced with the war news. St. Louis Poles prayed that Nazi oppression of Poland would end, but eyed the advance of Russian troops nervously. Doubting that once inside Poland's borders the Russians would leave, more than one St. Louis Pole despaired that their mother country would ever be free. The news of D day elated those of French heritage in the area, who held a joyous parade and party to celebrate Bastille Day, July 14, in grateful recognition of the free French forces.

St. Louis Jews watched the situation in Europe with ever-growing dread. Many of their relatives and friends had seemed to simply vanish. The full horror of Hitler's "final solution" was not yet evident, but stories about Nazi treatment of the Jews already seemed to be beyond belief. On Rosh Hashanah Rabbi Julius Gordon of Shaare Emeth Temple told his congregation, "Freedom from fear is indispensable if mankind is to experience a new birth and a new arrival. More positively, fear must be replaced by faith."

The same evening in Leige, Belgium, twenty Jewish GIs, including Sgt. Walter Weinstein of St. Louis, helped to reopen a synagogue after five years of "living death" under the Nazis. Only a little over 200 Jews were left in Leige of an original population of 3,000. Every one of the survivors had been tortured or had lost friends and relatives through torture. Nazis had used the holy scrolls belonging to the synagogue to wipe their feet. Somehow the Rabbi had managed to hide

St. Louisans made flannel toys for British children. From left, Mrs. William Mayors, Mrs. L. F. Huffstot, and Mrs. Robert Fulton Perkins.

The Fighting French Relief Society in St. Louis was directed by Mrs. Paul Blackwelder.

five scrolls, which were still intact.

The 1944 World Series really began in April when the St. Louis Browns went on an eight-game winning streak. By the Fourth of July, the Browns were — incredibly — on top of the American League. After forty-three years of seeing nothing but the darkness of the cellar, the Browns were basking in the light of victory. True, other teams had

Vic Vac, a popular newspaper cartoonist, envisioned the "streetcar series" of 1944 turning St. Louis into a baseball-crazy city. The Cardinals faced the Browns in the World Series.

been badly depleted by the draft and enlistments, but their lack is not what gave the Browns the drive that kept them at or near first place all season.

Kyle Crichton wrote of the "unbelievable Browns," that "they have a rickety-looking pitching staff and an outfield that has the appearance of something discarded from the Salvation Army, but these are war times and the rest of the league is no better."

The Cardinals, on the other hand, had been National League leaders for years. They had won the World Series in 1942 and the pennant in 1943. And they still had Stan Musial. It was no surprise that they were also on top on the Fourth of July or that they had captured the pennant when the season ended.

During the last two weeks of the season, the Browns won eleven of the twelve games they played. On October 2 the crowd at Sportsman's Park went wild when the Browns defeated the New York Yankees to clinch the American League pennant. October 2-9 was declared "Baseball Week" in St. Louis and no one could escape the epidemic of

Dr. Edward A. Doisy, director of the department of biochemistry at Saint Louis University School of Medicine, won the Nobel Prize in 1944.

Saint Louis University Archives

baseball fever that hit the city.

Col. Curtis H. Lohr, while on leave from Saint Louis University's hospital unit in North Africa, described what listening to the games meant to St. Louisans far from home. "We listened hungrily to the broadcasts of the World Series games. Why, we could even hear the vendors crying their popcorn, chewing gum, and candy wares in the grandstand. Believe me, there was a lot of nostalgia in the hospital after those games."

St. Louis also won the "intellectual world series" in 1944. Dr. Edward A. Doisy, director of the department of biochemistry at Saint Louis University School of Medicine, and Dr. Joseph Erlanger, professor of physiology and medicine at Washington University, each won a Nobel Prize. (Doisy's actually was for 1943, but was awarded in 1944.)

Edward Doisy was born in Hume, Illinois, in 1893. He attended the University of Illinois and Harvard University, where he received the Ph.D. in 1920. He joined the faculty of Washington University in 1919 and was lured to Saint Louis University in 1924. Doisy was intrigued by several biochemical reactions in the body, especially those involving uric acid, insulin, the inorganic components of the blood, and female sex hormones. But it was his work with the isolation of Vitamin K that won him the Nobel. In 1936 he began his research in conjunction with Dr. Henrik Dam of Denmark, who also won a Nobel Prize, and together they worked out the properties of this vitamin, which is necessary to the coagulation of blood.

Joseph Erlanger was born in 1874 in San Francisco and studied chemistry at the University of California. In 1899 he received an M.D. degree from Johns Hopkins, where he worked in the physiology department until 1906. After a few years at the newly-established University of Wisconsin Medical School, Erlanger moved to St. Louis and Washington University. At first Erlanger's primary interest was in the physiology of blood circulation, and he invented a sphygomomanometer to measure blood pressure. He also devised the "Erlanger clamp" which blocked the conduction of impulses in nerve bundles.

In 1921 Erlanger began a collaboration with Dr. Herbert S. Gasser, with whom he shared the Nobel, investigating the properties and functions of nerve fibers. They discovered that nerve trunks contain fibers that conduct impulses at three different rates. It was this discovery that brought Erlanger and Gasser the coveted award.

The demands of defense production encouraged the development of technology, if not of pure science. A research chemist with Alcoa on the east side, Ralph W. Brown, developed a limestone-sinter process which extracted aluminum oxide from ore by heating it. In 1944 Alcoa announced the presence of their plant in Illinois, which had been top secret until then, and stated it had seven gigantic kilns to use for the sintering process. The metal that resulted from the process was used for submarines and aircraft, since both needed lightweight metals. Aluminum ore was provided by the Aluminum Ore Company, also of the east side, which obtained its product in Arkansas.

Another St. Louis chemist was in the news during the year. Lt. Allan Barney, formerly with Anheuser-Busch, helped restore production in a brewery in Naples which had been wrecked by the Germans before they left. He wrote home about the experience, "Can you feature this? Right in the middle of things, I get back to my old work."

That fall the election began to look as if it might be close. Dewey was an energetic campaigner, and Roosevelt had to rely on the abilities of the untested Truman for his campaign. When Dewey came to St. Louis at the end of October, the city welcomed him with a ticker tape parade. That evening an old fashioned torchlight parade, complete with cowbells and high school band, accompanied Dewey to Kiel Auditorium where he delivered a major address. Charging the Democrats with corruption and sympathy for communism, Dewey reveled in the cheers of his audience. In the balcony, young women in white dresses sat so that they spelled out D-E-W-E-Y.

Despite the enthusiasm for Dewey in St. Louis, a straw poll at (Theodore) Roosevelt High School showed FDR ahead two to one. A heavy voter turnout on November 11 confirmed their preference. Despite the pull of the Democrat Roosevelt, Republican Kaufmann easily beat his opponent, Patrick J. Burke, for the office of mayor. Forrest C. Donnell became Missouri's new U.S. Senator, and Philip Donnelly was elected governor.

Soon after the election St. Louisans had a real reason to celebrate. The ads trumpeted, "It's gay! Gala! Glamorous! — The greatest event since the St. Louis Fair!" It was the world premiere of the movie *Meet Me in St. Louis,* held at Loew's Theater on November 22. Author Sally

Parades and hoopla for Thomas E. Dewey couldn't deliver the city's votes to the GOP. President Roosevelt won an unprecedented fourth term.

Benson, who had written the short story that was the basis for the MGM movie, was in town for the premiere. St Louis "feels like home to me and always will," she said.

As a girl, Benson had lived at 5135 Kensington Avenue (an address immortalized by one of the songs in the film), and most of the events of the movie had "almost" happened to her. "It's the way we wished we looked," she said, rather than a cinema verite presentation. It chronicled a turn-of-the-century life that was almost idyllic and culminated in the World's Fair of 1904. (The Bensons left St. Louis in 1910 for New York City.)

The premiere was SRO with an audience of four thousand — two thousand were turned away. St. Louis drama critic William Inge called the movie, which starred Judy Garland and Margaret O'Brien, Mary Astor, and Margery Main, "captivating" and "as full of memories as a trunk full of old souvenirs."

Despite the hoopla around the movie, St. Louis' third wartime Thanksgiving was a somber holiday. Too many of its dining tables had empty chairs. There were few shortages this year — food was plentiful and pockets were full of coins, but still there was an ache for those whom, it seemed, would never come home.

The only shortage of consequence during 1944 was a cigarette shortage in the last two months of the year. Panic buying resulted in empty racks and vending machines. A black market in tobacco sprang up at

John B. Sullivan and wife, Leonor, celebrate his victory as U.S. Representative (11th district) the morning after the election.

One of America's favorite movies premiered in St. Louis in 1944. Its pleasant, nostalgic look at the 1904 World's Fair reminded the nation of better days.

once in response.

As Christmas approached, the news from Europe was the worst yet. American troops were trapped at Bastogne in the grueling Battle of the Bulge. The Nazis were summoning up strength for a final offensive and the American GIs were badly weakened by hunger and cold. No one felt very merry.

Almost half a million Christmas packages were sent through the St. Louis post office to those in the service overseas. The government bragged that ninety-eight percent got through intact. A 1944 directive stated that V-mail with lipstick would no longer be delivered. A SWAK letter ("sealed with a kiss") frequently smeared and caused problems with the photo equipment used for reducing.

As 1945 approached even the most optimistic could see that there would be another year of war. St. Louisans were urged over and over to return to defense plants, to sacrifice their own careers just a little while longer and "bring the boys home in '45." Mayor Kaufmann's year-end message to St. Louisans summed up the urgency:

"This is a new war! We on the home front must recognize that fact! St. Louis Men and Women: This is your war. These are your boys. Back them up by taking your war job now — and stick to it!"

THE FOURTH YEAR — 1945
VICTORY

AS THE NEW YEAR OPENED the mood of the country was grim. Military leaders had been certain that the war would end shortly after D day — but D day had been six months ago and victory still seemed a long time away. Both the Germans and the Japanese were fighting with a fury that seemed superhuman. The only answer the Allies could come up with was to give them more: more air strikes, more bombs, more fighting men, more bullets.

In his State of the Union address President Roosevelt asked for more, too — for a stepped-up draft, not only for men into the military, but also for nurses and defense plant workers. The 4,000,000 men who had been judged 4-F the first time around prepared themselves for another exam. The armed forces needed another couple of million men right away and there was nowhere else to find them. St. Louis nurses responded at once to Roosevelt's plea for help. The recruiting office at Malcolm Bliss Hospital reported a one hundred percent increase in the number of enlistments.

The seriousness of the situation was emphasized by the casualty lists, which were growing daily as fighting on both fronts intensified. The February battle for Iwo Jima was the bloodiest of the war, and the War Mobilization Office made the somber prediction that in March more men would be in combat than at any time since Pearl Harbor. As many as 3,000 Americans were being wounded or killed each day. But ordnance production was lower than it had been since the war began. The momentum at home was being lost.

Defense plant employers found that after an initial surge of applications following the president's address, the number of workers seeking jobs dropped off. Employers offered bonuses, promised summer vaca-

A shortage of war workers led to a shortage of shells at the front.

tions, and hinted at other benefits. They courted the handicapped and sought out women. Day-care programs for children were expanded and upgraded. But still there were few applicants.

Then Mayor Kaufmann's Labor and Management Committee came up with a plan to transfer workers from nonessential to essential industries. Their original jobs would be protected, they promised, waiting in mothballs until the end of the war. But the logistics of shuffling people around and keeping factories open without a production line met with little enthusiasm and the plan became too difficult for the committee to implement.

A feeling of desperation gripped defense contractors — the army was crying for 800 million cartridges a month, but rows of machines stood empty at the ordnance factories because there were not enough employees to operate them. The need for Superfortresses and bomb

A door-to-door canvass for war workers was threatened in St. Louis, but it never materialized.

casings was at its peak — bombing raids on Japan and Berlin required hundreds of planes and tons of bombs — yet eight area foundries were closed by labor walkouts and no amount of patriotic rhetoric could make workers walk back in. A black steelworker who went on strike told a journalist, "The white man gives me a chance now because he needs steel for the war. But what will he do to me after the war?" Thousands of cynical — or realistic — workers asked the same question. After being used for four years, they could see that they were expendable. As soon as the war was over, they could be back in unemployment lines.

In March J. Wesley McAfee, Union Electric chief, headed a drive to find 27,500 additional war workers in the area. Two hundred and seventy plants needed workers. Newspapers, billboards, radio, and motion pictures were enlisted in the campaign. The drive began with a kickoff rally at Kiel Auditorium where seven heroes of Bastogne and a twenty-seven-piece military band tried to whip up support for the war effort. Some 200,000 circulars were distributed throughout the community urging people to register with the employment service. Movies at 105 theaters were interrupted with pleas from defense plants. The *Star-Times* even ran a step-by-step photo essay to show how easy it was to get a job: At 8:26 A.M., an applicant walked into the U.S. Employ-

Even strong appeals to patriotism couldn't keep restless defense workers on the line in 1945.

ment Service; by 10:30 she was on the line at Century Electric. The up-shot of the campaign was that 5,000 new workers were found — one-fifth of the number needed.

The problem was not simply one of finding more workers, it was also one of keeping workers on the job. Absenteeism at Continental Can was twenty-seven percent and it was almost as high at other defense plants. Production lagged well behind schedules. Workers were asked to sign — and to honor — pledges, which said:

"I hereby assure General MacArthur and Admiral Nimitz that I, unless unforeseen circumstances beyond my control arise, will stay on the job in our plant as long as I am needed to help produce whatever is required for our armed forces on any fighting front around the world."

Nonetheless, strikes spread like the measles from one plant to

· *This GI's boots, leggings, jacket, helmet, helmet liner, sleeping bag, and tent could have been made in St. Louis. The city's garment industry had contracts for all such items.*

another. Half of Curtiss-Wright's 12,000 employees went on strike for two crucial weeks in April. The president of General Cable flew in from New York to address his employees here in an attempt to prevent a threatened strike because the company was about to hire 400 blacks. He pointed out that the forefathers of most of the employees fled from discrimination in Europe. "It would be a crime for you to create here the very situation your forefathers left Europe to avoid," he said.

One strike which dragged on for weeks threatened the troops in the field as much as a lack of ammunition — a strike at International Shoe Company. St. Louis' shoe industry made millions of pairs of shoes, combat boots, and submarine sandals for the military, 50 million pairs in 1943 alone. At its peak, International produced 35,000 pairs of shoes per day. Each soldier was given three pairs of footwear. Since he spent most of his time on his feet, even three pairs didn't last long, particularly in the jungles of the South Pacific or in the mud of Italy.

Special shoe-repair units followed combat troops. When the repairs needed were beyond their capacity, the shoes or boots were sent back to huge repair plants at Hannibal, Missouri, and at Alcatraz prison, where as many as 20,000 pairs of worn shoes arrived each day. There they were repaired or rebuilt if possible, disinfected, and returned to the front for another GI.

On September 22 Gen. Leif J. Sverdrup, head of the consulting engineering firm of Sverdrup & Parcel Company, wrote home from Jaure, New Guinea, "Hope my shoes hold out. Had two pairs when I started — one is gone completely and the other not so hot. When you have to cross streams all of the time by wading across, your shoes soon rot away. Even though they are made by International Shoe Co., as mine are."

At Brown Shoe Company, a new type of boot was developed with buckles, which fit over the trousers. This meant that old-style leggings were no longer needed. (But until the new boots were in wide use, the Bray Company of St. Louis turned out 1,250,000 pairs of leggings.) Brown also made extra-wide military shoes for the Russians. To avoid frostbite in their bitterly cold winters, Russian soldiers wore several pairs of socks made of grass and wool, which required an enormous boot.

Johansen Brothers Shoe Company also manufactured military footwear, and Landis Shoe Machinery Company made machinery for making and repairing shoes. Protecting the all-important foot soldier's "dogs" was crucial to the success of the march to Berlin. So was protecting the rest of him. Half of the helmets used in combat were made in St. Louis by Schlueter Manufacturing Company. Paul K. Weil Company made helmet liners and Rawlings Sporting Goods Company made the special helmets for tank personnel. (All three companies won the Army-Navy "E" for excellence.)

Tons of uniforms, from WAC blouses to ack-ack jackets, nurses' whites and defense plant coveralls, bell-bottomed trousers and gob hats were made by the St. Louis garment industry. Angelica Jacket Company produced 25 million combat fatigue outfits, the shapeless uniforms made famous by Bill Mauldin's cartoon characters, Willie and Joe. Other manufacturers turned out turned out pup tents, bedrolls, mattresses for ambulances and transport planes, and pillows.

Foster Brothers Manufacturing Company made steel cots for the army and ship berths and fittings for the navy. Their bunks went into LSTs, aircraft carriers, destroyers, destroyer escorts, and hospital ships. Tons of parachutes were made in St. Louis. Paul K. Weil Co. made flare parachutes with 60mm M-83 mine flares. Others had ground signal flares. Nixdorff-Krein made the "bloomer chains" for paratroopers pants to keep them from riding up, and International Shoe made paratroopers' boots.

Many bunks, such as these built for an LST, were manufactured in St. Louis.

Curiously, the strike epidemic of 1945 spread to Jefferson Barrack, where over 300 Nazi prisoners laid down their tools and refused to work in January because a fellow POW had been disciplined. They were given bread and water and, after several days of this diet, decided to go back to work.

About one hundred German prisoners were then working as farm laborers in St. Louis County near Chesterfield. One night Walter Winchell mentioned on his radio broadcast that "nothing is to prevent them from blowing up the Weldon Spring plant." Plant officials responded immediately by saying that explosives were not even stored there, but were shipped out as fast as possible. Two climb-proof fences and an armed patrol protected the area, and the buildings had been arranged so that extensive damage would be impossible in the unlikely event a saboteur should get through the defenses. About fifty other German prisoners worked for the Army Corps of Engineers and lived in a boat at the foot of Arsenal Street.

In 1944 two Nazi prisoners escaped from Fort Leonard Wood and fears were raised again about the loyalty of some members of the German community in St. Louis. But an extensive FBI investigation of alleged ties stretching from the fatherland to St. Louis showed that practically none existed. In the spring of 1945 the FBI announced that membership in the German-American Bund at its peak (1939) in St. Louis was only 200, and there were never more than fifty in Nazi uniform during the three years of its existence, 1937-40. Bund members did distribute Nazi literature, but did not engage in sabotage, and apparently never seriously advocated it. They did, however, collect information on local war plants which was turned over to German authorities. The headquarters for the Bund during its short life here was Camp Duetsch Horst on the Meramec River, where the Swastika flew alongside the American flag and where children were taught the German language and culture. When war broke out in Europe St. Louis Bund leaders returned to Germany and the movement died out here.

One St. Louisan was definitely no fan of the Nazis. On January 8, 1945, near Kayserberg, France, Tech. Sgt. Russell E. Dunham single-handedly attacked three Nazi machine guns. From a mattress cover he made a white robe for camouflage against the snow and armed himself to the hilt. He carried twelve carbine magazines and snagged a dozen hand grenades in his belt, suspenders, and buttonholes.

As the army report states,

His platoon 35 yards behind him, T/Sgt. Dunham crawled 75 yards under heavy direct fire toward the timbered emplacement shielding the left machinegun. As he jumped to his feet 10 yards from the gun and charged forward, machinegun fire tore through his camouflage robe and a rifle bullet seared a 10-inch gash across his back sending him spinning 15 yards down hill into the snow. When the indomitable sergeant sprang to his feet to renew his 1-man assault, a German egg grenade landed beside him. He kicked it aside, and as it exploded 5 yards away, shot and killed the German machinegunner and assistant gunner. His carbine empty, he jumped into the emplacement and hauled out the third member of the gun crew by the collar. Although his back wound was causing him excruciating pain and blood was seeping through his white coat, T/Sgt. Dunham proceeded 50 yards through a storm of automatic and rifle fire to attack the second machinegun. Twenty-five yards from the emplacement he hurled 2 grenades, destroying the gun and its crew; then fired down into the supporting foxholes with his carbine, dispatching and dispersing the enemy riflemen."

Dunham continued the attack with incredible intensity. At fifteen yards from the nest, he staggered forward, lobbed off his hand grenades and killed the machine gun crew. An enemy rifleman fired at him point-blank and missed. Dunham killed him instead. The rest of the Germans were driven from their foxholes. The final tally showed nine Germans killed, seven wounded and two captured. For this act, T/Sgt. Russell Dunham received the Medal of Honor for ''conspicuous gallantry and intrepidity at risk of life above and beyond the call to duty.''

The portable Bailey bridge, built by Stupp Brothers Bridge and Iron Company,
was used in both the European and Pacific theaters of war.

As Allied troops advanced across France, Belgium, and into Germany, they found that most of the bridges had been destroyed, either by their own bombs or by the retreating German army. Two St. Louis companies provided ingenious stopgap measures to keep the Allies going.

Mississippi Valley Structural Steel Company constructed 114 portable railroad bridges in a little over four months. (The British had turned out only fifty bridges in a year and a half.) These precision-gauge bridges were built to connect with European variable-gauge railroad tracks, which meant that tolerances were measured in thousandths of an inch. To reduce assembly time to a minimum, the edges of plates and parts were machined, "insuring rapid and accurate assembly of the various piece parts in the welding jigs," reported *Commerce* magazine. "This also reduced to a minimum the amount of shrinkage and warpage from welding and speeded up the entire program."

The Mississippi Valley bridges were used primarily in Europe. Those built by Stupp Bros. Bridge & Iron Company were used in both theaters. Stupp built Bailey bridges, named for the British engineer who designed them. Unlike the railroad bridges, they were flexible in assembly. Because they had so many parts they took longer to assemble than other bridges and were almost rejected by the army. When the

Mississippi Valley Structural Steel Co. made these temporary bridges to replace those blown up in the European campaign.

T23 tank was designated for use, the Bailey bridge was reconsidered. The T23 was 124 inches wide and the Bailey had a clear deck of 129 inches, making it the only portable bridge wide enough for the new tank. In 1944 a Bailey bridge 150 inches widewas designed, which increased its serviceability even more.

Some factories had been released from defense contracts in 1944 and had begun manufacturing civilian goods again. Nonetheless, few new appliances, sporting goods, or tools were available in early 1945. The cigarette shortage of 1944 increased to the point where they were rationed at fifteen cigarettes per day per adult in January. This resulted in a tremendous black market operation.

The beer shortage also became more serious in 1945. Four of the major breweries in town (Anheuser-Busch, Griesedieck, Hyde Park, and Falstaff) routinely shipped fifteen percent of their suds to the troops overseas, which meant that about 800,000 cases of beer were not available for St. Louis consumers.

And a severe meat, poultry, and fish shortage surfaced again in March. The supply of meat was cut twelve percent for civilians, to the lowest point of the war. Virtually all chicken, canned or fresh, was set aside for the army. This caused a hardship on orthodox Jews who used chicken necks or wings to symbolize the Paschal Lamb during Passover. Rabbinical authorities okayed the use of substitutes for the ceremony, but many black market chickens found their way to Passover tables.

A full-page advertisement which appeared in newspapers in the spring, sponsored by the Mayrose Packing Company, explained the problem: The St. Louis packing industry was required to reserve sixty percent of its choice beef for the government, seventy percent of its utility beef, fifty percent of its pork, forty to fifty percent of its lamb, fifty percent of its veal, and seventy-five percent of its lard. There wasn't much left over for civilians.

Many St. Louis area companies provided food for the military. Among them were Absogood Packing Co., Anheuser-Busch, Fischer Meat Co., Commercial Coffee Co., Chester B. Franz Co., Hunter Packing Co., Krey Foods, Inc., Nestle, G. S. Suppiger, and S & E Glazer Packing Co., as well as Mayrose. As the army itself said, "The regular serving of palatable food is the greatest single factor in building and maintaining high spirit and morale." Unfortunately, nothing was so heartily disliked about the army as its chow, despite the best efforts of the Quartermaster Corps.

The challenge that the Corps faced was to produce field rations that contained the requisite amount of fats, carbohydrates, proteins, minerals and vitamins, that were lightweight, had a long shelf life, were protected from the elements, rough handling, and insect contamination, and that were "palatable." The task was all but impossible.

The complaint most often heard was about the monotony of rations, whatever the variety — A, B, C, D, K, jungle, mountain, 5-in-1, 10-in-1, or AAC. Because combat rations (C and K) had to be carried without refrigeration and eaten without preparation, they had to be nonperishable. Because they had to be high in calories and high in protein, their diversity was further limited. In fact, field rations most often turned out to be the ubiquitous Spam or something called "meat and vegetables" (or "hash or stew," depending on the size and quality of the meat). A biscuit, cereal bar, candy bar, instant coffee and a few other amenities, including a packet of matches supplied by Universal Match Company, were a part of the package.

In 1944 the Quartermaster Corps added new menus, which included chicken, ham and eggs, frankfurters and beans, and potatoes. This led to corresponding shortages at home, even of potatoes.

St. Louis companies produced more than food for the Quartermaster Corps. S. G. Adams made mess kits, Charter Oak Stove & Range Co. made Army field ranges and thermal insulators for food storage, Curtis Manufacturing Co. made refrigeration equipment, Hussman-Ligionier turned out self-contained refrigeration units, and Majestic Manufacturing Co. made heavy-duty ranges for Victory ships.

Portable ranges and galleys were made by Charter Oak Stove and Majestic Manufacturing companies.

The most severe coal shortage of the war hit the nation in the early months of 1945. The use of coal in homes was cut by twenty percent. In an effort to save coal for more essential tasks, a nationwide "brownout" was initiated at the end of January. In St. Louis 4,000 outdoor signs were darkened, as only 60-watt light bulbs were allowed for theaters, gas stations, and stores.

In February the War Mobilization Office announced a midnight curfew for all restaurants, night spots, and sports arenas, again to save coal. St. Louis late-night establishments agreed to comply with the ruling, but the first week it was in effect, fifty-three violations were recorded. Three hundred restaurants were affected by the curfew, including those in hotels. Patronage at the restaurants and bars of the Koplar hotels — the Park Plaza, Chase, Congress, and Forest Park — dropped between thirty and forty percent, said Harold Koplar, managing director. Only all-night eateries which served war workers and no liquor were exempt from the curfew. Proving that the clientele were war workers required filing forms and affidavits, adding to the bureaucratic maze that all government controls engendered. Eventually, Washington officials discovered that the curfew was hurting morale rather than saving coal and began to ease restrictions even before the war ended.

In January the forces of Gen. Douglas MacArthur invaded Luzon in the Philippines on their return to Manila. As American troops fanned

Lt. Beulah Greenwalt, the "angel of Bataan" who was immortalized as "Peggy" in the book They Were Expendable, *was overjoyed to return to Missouri after a harrowing ordeal as a POW.*

out across the island, they were joined by GIs who had given their Japanese captors the slip and managed to survive. Sgt. Raymond Hunt, Jr., of St. Louis, escaped from the Bataan death march and had lived in the Luzon hills for two years.

He told reporters about the march, "I saw two sick men bayoneted because they couldn't keep up with the column. At long intervals we'd be given rest periods. The Japs would herd us into small inclosures where there wasn't even room enough to lie down. Then, after a few minutes, the march would start again.

"I had plenty of chances to escape, but during the first ten days I was too sick to try it. But on the tenth day I realized that I was near the end of my strength. To collapse meant death by clubbing. So I jumped into a ditch and lay still, hoping the guards hadn't seen me." Hunt crawled away when it seemed safe to do so and made his way up into the hills.

The "angels of Bataan and Corregidor" were among those freed from Japanese prison camps on Luzon. Three of these nurses were from the St. Louis area — 2nd Lt. Aldolpha Meyer, 2nd Lt. Minnie J. Breese, and Lt. Beulah Greenwalt. Greenwalt was the "Peggy" of the popular book *They Were Expendable.* She returned to her childhood home in Licking, Missouri, early in March. Feted by the Chamber of Commerce, Lieutenant Greenwalt spoke for all liberated prisoners when she told a standing-room-only audience at a Chamber luncheon, "If there could be a happier day than the day of liberation, it was the day we again saw our own homeland."

American POWs were being liberated in Europe, too. As they returned home they brought messages of hope to families of those still being held captive. And they told stories of bitter deprivation. Lt. Robert J. Baumann of St. Louis said, "All we talked about in those

These grim faces mirror the anxiety and sorrow felt on hearing of Roosevelt's death a month before the fall of Germany.

long dreary days was hamburger and chicken.''

A special breed of vultures preyed on the families of those missing in action or imprisoned. Calling themselves spiritualists or mediums, they exploited the anxiety and grief of those waiting at home by claiming to have certain knowledge of the whereabouts of loved ones. Fortunetellers, clairvoyants, spirit mediums, seers, necromancers, and palmists were illegal in St. Louis, but most of these prophets got around the law by using the title reverend and calling their establishments churches.

By April the news from both theaters was heartening. The Allies were at last on an aggressive and fast-moving offensive. General George S. Patton had pierced the Siegfried Line and was only miles from Berlin. The Red Army was in its eastern outskirts. Then, on April 12, 1945, came another blow to the American people.

The headlines told the story: President Roosevelt was dead. An editorial called him ''another Moses — a man who led his people to the frontiers of a promised land, but who was himself denied passage across its border.'' All political differences were forgotten as the nation grieved. Sorrow spread throughout St. Louis.

President Truman declared April 14 a day of national mourning. In St. Louis 4,000 people attended an 11 A.M. memorial service at Soldier's Memorial. They shivered in 53-degree weather as a cold rain

Harry S. Truman said he felt that the stars and moon had fallen on him when he learned that he was the new president of the United States. Watching him take the oath of office are his wife, Bess, and daughter, Margaret.

fell from drab skies and the mournful sound of taps echoed through the quiet streets.

Attorney Jacob M. Lashly delivered the eulogy and someone quoted from a Roosevelt speech, delivered here in 1936, ''We best honor the memory of those dead by striving for peace so that the terror of the days of war will be with us no longer.'' On April 15 2,000,000 pounds of clothes were collected for the destitute in Europe as a gesture of commitment to Roosevelt's ideals.

St. Louisans wished the new president well. The St. Louis Metropolitan Church Federation wrote to him that the church people of St. Louis were praying for him. Truman replied, ''I am sure the task ahead will seem less difficult because I shall have the prayers of all those good friends about whom you write. . . . Their thought of me in this special way means more to me than I can say!''

In the months ahead, the Roosevelt administration gradually became the Truman administration and several St. Louisans moved to Washington at Truman's request. Charles O. Ross, the 59-year old contributing editor to the *Post-Dispatch* who had won a Pulitzer Prize in 1936, became Truman's press secretary. Col. Harry H. Vaughan became his military aide and James K. Vardaman, his naval aide.

Margaret Hickey, left, served on the wartime manpower commission. President Truman appointed her to the U.S. delegation to the United Nations after the war.

Truman appointed his old pal, Bob Hannegan, postmaster general, and Alfred Schindler, undersecretary of commerce. St. Louis banker John W. Snyder became the federal loan administrator, Margaret Hickey was named a consultant to the U.S. delegation to the United Nations, and Emerson Electric president Stuart Symington joined the surplus property board as chairman.

On April 30 Munich was captured and in Italy Benito Mussolini was executed, stirring reports that the war had ended. The next day, May 1, Nazi radio reported that Adolf Hitler was dead and that he had died a "hero." St. Louisans doubted it. They greeted the news of Hitler's death (which later was revealed as an ignominious suicide) with "Oh, yeah? Show me!" and even the extras didn't convince them. "People have been killing Hitler so long in their minds," said one commentator, "that his actual death is anti-climactic." Ordering an extra round of drinks in a bar was the extent of the celebration here.

The Russian army had battled its way into the heart of Berlin by May 2, when the city surrendered. *Post-Dispatch* correspondent Virginia Irwin was illegally in Berlin as it fell. She filed an exclusive with the *Post:* "As I write, the Russians' artillery is pounding the heart of the city with a barrage I have never heard equaled in an American battle. The earth shakes. The air stinks of cordite and the dead."

Everyone was waiting anxiously for V-E day. After Berlin fell,

Mayor Al Kaufmann congratulates the Civil Defense Corps for their work dur-ing the early years of the war. From left, Mayor Kaufmann; John D. Martin of the national OCD office; St. Louis OCD coordinator Col. Harry D. McBride; J. Wesley McAfee, executive of the Service Corps; and Commander Nelson Cunliff.

Americans knew that victory could be declared at any minute. Premature announcements came regularly over the wire service and people didn't know what to believe. Mayor Kaufmann declared that the only authentic news of V-E day would come from his office. The telephone company urged people not to reach for their telephone to check the news, but to listen to the radio. The already overburdened phone system couldn't stand an avalanche of calls.

On May 4 the Nazis surrendered Denmark and Holland, but there was still no word on an unconditional surrender. The mood of the city was cautious and sober. Then, finally, on May 8 it was official.

Bells, whistles and horns sounded the news at 8 A.M.: Victory in Europe! But after the bells stopped pealing, a "sabbath quiet" descended on the area. Five thousand people attended a city-wide prayer service at Soldiers Memorial in the morning. Shops and businesses closed for the day, but defense plants kept their assembly lines moving, and war workers stopped only momentarily to reflect on meaning of V-E day. The war in Europe had taken 27,000,000 lives and trillions of dollars. Cities had been demolished, artwork destroyed, families devastated, lives ruined. Now it was over.

The city turned its attention from Europe to the Pacific. As the war effort began to wind down, St. Louis provided almost a mirror image of the mobilization of 1941-42. The Red Cross blood bank was the first to announce that it would close, then the Office of Civil Defense said it would go out of business. Layoffs at defense plants began. As many as twenty thousand workers received notice of termination within a week of V-E day, just as they had feared. Four thousand employees of U.S. Cartridge who were terminated held a mass meeting to ask for severance pay and unemployment compensation for two months, while they looked for other work. The answer was unequivocally no. The army decided to turn the ordnance plant into a records center to house the mountains of paperwork resulting from building an organization of eleven million men and women.

Curtiss-Wright began laying off workers on May 26, as expected. A new Curtiss-Wright plane, the experimental Ascender XP-44, had been flown at Lambert and Scott fields early in the year. Its radical new design made it appear to fly backward, but it was also highly maneuverable and very fast. Its engine and propeller were in the rear, so the guns in the nose did not have to fire in synch with the propeller, making the operation easier.

In spite of its advantages, the Ascender received a cool reception among the military. Still, Curtiss-Wright had contracts for the Commando and Helldiver and business appeared to be booming. Then, abruptly, in the first week in June, Curtiss-Wright officials announced that the plant would close within the month and 11,000 employees would be dismissed. Chamber of Commerce president George Smith was stunned.

Smith, Mayor Kaufmann, and other St. Louis leaders had been making plans for the postwar development of the city for nearly two years. All the hopes depended on full employment. In January Kaufmann unveiled plans for a $63,385,000 postwar public works program, which included trunk line sanitary sewers, levee improvements, land use changes, new streets and highways, a rapid transit system, a new airport, and new housing. (Plans for a downtown airport were scuttled when an army B-25 bomber rammed into the Empire State building in New York City in late July. Airplanes and tall buildings seemed too dangerous a combination.) An "anti-slum" committee was named, which began talking about urban renewal — a new St. Louis was to emerge.

Few city improvements had been made during the depression and practically none during the war. St. Louis was ready for a renewal. Thousands of new residents not accustomed to urban living had flocked to the city seeking defense jobs. They had jammed themselves into substandard housing, which had become even more dilapidated.

Studies made during 1945 showed that many of St. Louis' children were underfed and poor nutrition had led to poor health. Pupils in the St. Louis public school system averaged two years below the national norm for scholastic achievement.

City officials hoped that area businesses would lead the way to prosperity. Arthur C. Drefs, chairman of the board of the Chamber and president of McQuay-Norris, called for a thirty-five percent expansion in local business to compensate for the loss of government contracts. Famous Barr, Stix Baer and Fuller, and Scruggs announced that they planned to expand into shopping arcades away from the downtown area, a novel concept at the time.

Southwestern Bell also planned a large ($34,000,000) postwar expansion. Envisioning future nation-wide networks, Bell hoped to help develop the new technology of television. (KSD-TV had begun broadcasting a few hours a day in 1944. All television at that time consisted of local, live broadcasting and an occasional film.) And Bell promised that new telephones would at last be available in spring of 1946.

Before the war St. Louis was a city of small businesses. The "mom and pop" grocery store, the family clothing store, and the factory with a handful of employees were the rule. Only 127 companies of more than 2,500 in the metropolitan area could be classified as big business, that is, employing over 500 people. Small businesses had wrestled with burdensome taxation, endless restrictions, confusing and conflicting regulations, and rationing during the war. The boom had been exciting and expansion was good, but the price was high. The area's economy had been almost completely dominated and controlled by the government for four years. Now, thought business owners, it was time to return to free enterprise.

But it was impossible to return to a pre-war state. Too many changes had been made and too many expectations for the good life had been raised. Rev. Bernard W. Dempsey, S.J., regent of the School of Commerce and Finance at Saint Louis University, predicted that a "shore leave atmosphere" would predominate after the war. Social changes would continue at a tremendous rate, inflation and economic instability would mean insecurity, and none of the old rules would apply.

A few weeks after V-E day it was promised that by the first of July civilian goods would again be available. The first postwar refrigerator and the first Nash automobile were duly photographed as harbingers of a trend. But in fact, the first new cars for the general population were fifteen months away, new sewing machines wouldn't be produced for nine months, and vacuum cleaners still had four months before they were for sale. One shortage that popped up in the last days of the war had men gnashing their teeth — men's shorts disappeared from the shelves. "We can't keep them in stock," said one merchant. In

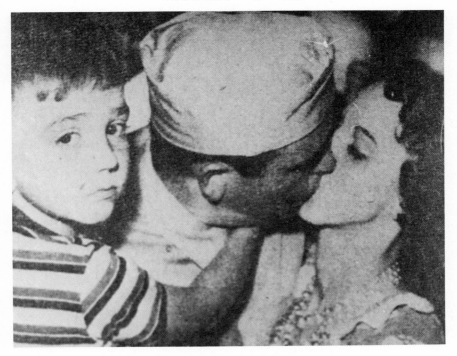

"Welcome home, Dad." (I think.)

desperation, some men turned to wearing women's underpants, first "cutting off the lace."

A bumper crop of peaches during the summer gave St. Louisans their first food surplus in years. But a shortage of canning sugar meant that only a few could be preserved — the rest had to be eaten at once or spoil. Despite the ingenious new recipes developed for using peaches, they became such a glut on the market that some homemakers vowed they would never get near a peach again.

In July the sugar shortage again became crucial. Quotas were cut back to sixty percent of 1941 levels. This cut, coupled with a seventy percent reduction in the amount of cooking fat allowed, forced many small bakeries out of business.

Within days of the announcement of victory in Europe, 2,000,000 men were mustered out of the service. On May 24 the first contingent of 7,000 Yanks arrived in New York harbor. They were followed by a steady stream of returning vets.

Reunions were joyous and thanksgiving was heartfelt. Then, within days of the homecoming, problems began to surface. The long separation had strained family relations. Children were introduced to "Dad," a man they didn't remember or didn't even know. Wives had

The reality of war — a wounded serviceman awaits a chance to walk again.

developed new interests and sometimes found new men friends while their husbands were gone. The vets had had experiences they couldn't — or didn't want — to share with their families. Often they seemed like strangers. Occasionally they brought with them new wives, "war brides," who had to adjust to American culture in a hurry.

Brig. Gen. George Shea, commander of Jefferson Barracks, said that returning servicemen should not be considered a "problem." "Some of the civilians will be more of a problem than servicemen," he insisted, and predicted that those who had served in combat would be mature, solid, and reliable citizens.

Many vets felt a need to stay in contact with other vets. The first American Legion Post of World War II vets was organized here in the spring of 1945. Al Londe, former Mizzou football player, walked into the southside YMCA office one day and said to the director, "Now that we have finished fighting, we know what we were fighting for, and we must keep fighting for it on the home front. Many of the boys who come back will be too old for a boys' club, but can't we a establish a Legion post?" They did and named it Hill-Millner, for Lt. Harry Hill, killed in France, and Marine Pvt. William G. Milner, killed in the South Pacific.

Hanger Artificial Limbs made thousands of prosthetic devices for injured combatants during the war.

Vets met frequently during the summer to air gripes about civilian life. The most pressing problem was finding shelter. In June the *Star-Times* described the plight of thousands of St. Louisans who spent each month "on a wearying march for a place to live." Five hundred renters were evicted each month and five thousand lived in "unliveable" quarters. "All I want is a place I can call home for me and my family," one vet lamented. But it wasn't available.

The next need was for a job. As the economy contracted, vets found that promises about jobs waiting for them at home were hollow. The U.S. Employment Service in St. Louis claimed that it had found jobs for 10,417 returning vets by the end of July, but thousands more were still unemployed. Many vets wanted an education or to upgrade their skills. They felt the government owed them a "G.I. Bill of Rights" to help them find a place in society again, and began to lobby their congressmen. (Eventually they got it.)

Vets also disliked the confusion of agencies that were created to help them. They called the Veterans Administration a mess and felt lost in its bureaucratic tangle. The VA hospital in St. Louis did not have enough beds for the returning wounded and its psychiatric facilities were practically nonexistent. The War Dads organization and the mayor's committee on the problems of returning vets worked to improve conditions at the hospital and to get quality medical care for

Creve Coeur was one of the first communities in the area to honor its war dead.

them.

The city had long been planning a memorial for its war dead. Architect Eugene J. Mackey, Jr., of Washington University was commissioned to design the plaza, which was to be located in the block next to the Soldiers Memorial. On July 4 the cornerstone for the city's memorial, the "Court of Honor," was laid by two soldiers who made it back. The names of all military personnel who died during World War II were carved into walls that enclose a garden. The names of those killed in Korea and Vietnam have since been added.

Throughout the spring of 1945, new words were being added to America's vocabulary: Buchenwald, Limburg, Thekla, Nordhausen, Bad Orb, Hammelberg, Kassel, Belsen, Ohrdruf, Ducerstadt, Dachau. . . . On May 27 the city in conjunction with the army began showing films of Nazi atrocities, which had been taken as concentration camps were liberated. The films were shown at Kiel Auditorium every two hours throughout the day and evening. It was hoped that everyone in the area over the age of sixteen would see them, so it could be said with some finality, "Never again!" War workers were bused to the auditorium for special showings. Most people were shocked and appalled by the films. However Gerald L. K. Smith's new magazine, *The Eleventh Hour,* which was being published in St. Louis, doubted the truth of Nazi atrocities, claiming that stories about them were just more propaganda put out by the "international Jewish conspiracy."

Gen. Omar Bradley, a native Missourian, addresses a packed Chamber of Commerce luncheon in the Gold Room of the Jefferson Hotel.

In mid-June General Omar Bradley visited his native state of Missouri and St. Louisans turned out in great numbers to welcome him home and to salute his heroism. Bradley's troops had captured Bizerte in North Africa, broken the Nazi hold on Tunisia, stormed **beaches of Normandy on D day, crashed through the German line at** St. Lo, held the south side of the Belgian "bulge," finally flattening it, and were the first across the Rhine in the final push toward Berlin.

General Eisenhower stopped briefly in St. Louis the next week on his way back to Abilene, Kansas, where he was also feted as a hero. Ike had won a lot of friends in St. Louis when he had taken time from overseeing the European campaign to write to fifth grader Edward Merkel in February, commending him for collecting fifty pounds of scrap paper and "doing your share toward furthering the war effort."

The "Mighty Seventh" Loan Drive began the week after V-E day with a goal of $156,772,436, or an average of $50 from each area resident. It was the most poorly subscribed drive of all and didn't come close to its goal. Bond sales moved at "a snail's pace." An Anheuser-Busch ad promoting the drive summed up the mood of the community, "Wearily we roll along . . . But we'll keep on rolling."

Even though area officials tried to keep workers interested in producing war materiel, everyone knew the war was nearly over. How could Japan take much more? Almost every day throughout July Superforts bombed its industrial cities. On July 10 some 1,800 planes bombarded the islands. "Tokyo in Flames!" said headlines. "Osaka Blasted!" But even after a month of such punishment, the Japanese government turned down an ultimatum to surrender by refusing to acknowledge the Potsdam Declaration issued by Truman, Churchill, and Chiang

Dr. Arthur Holly Compton was one of the fathers of the atomic bomb and later chancellor of Washington University.

Arthur Holly Compton papers, Washington University Archives

Kai-shek on July 25.

On August 4 the United States informed Tokyo that twelve more Japanese cities would be served "death notices," and even worse torment was in store for its people unless it capitulated. There was no response.

Because this eventuality had been considered a possibility as early as 1942, the U.S. had begun to develop a "secret weapon," one so powerful that it would bring any enemy — no matter how adamant — to its knees at once. The weapon was the atomic bomb, two thousand times more powerful than the biggest of the blockbuster bombs.

Developing the bomb required a marriage of science and technology and the enlistment of some of the best brains in the country. As many as 5,000 St. Louisans worked on the Manhattan project, as it was called, as scientists, engineers, technicians, skilled labor and secretaries, in St. Louis and in the various installations around the country where pieces of the bomb were made and assembled — Oak Ridge, Tennessee; Hanford, Washington; and Los Alamos, New Mexico.

In the spring of 1942 Mallinckrodt Chemical Works was assigned the task of refining crude uranium ore for the bomb. Shortly thereafter, it produced a test-tubeful of pure uranium dioxide. Within months, it was turning out one ton of dioxide a day. The world's first manmade atomic chain reaction, initiated at the University of Chicago on December 2, 1942, used fifty tons of Mallinckrodt's uranium oxide blocks. Monsanto Chemical Company also contributed expertise to the development of the bomb. Its most noted scientist, Dr. Charles A. Thomas, was involved in top secret work throughout the war.

Several St. Louisans paved the way for the atomic bomb. Dr. Arthur Holly Compton, who was later appointed chancellor of Washington University, supervised the University of Chicago physicists who

Washington University Archives

The cyclotron — or "atom smasher" — at Washington University.

worked on the bomb. Dr. Arthur Hughes, chairman of the physics department at Washington University, and Dr. Alexander S. Langsdorf, Jr., assistant physicist in the Mallinckrodt Institute of Radiology, worked with the "atom smasher," the cyclotron at WU, to provide information about atomic energy.

On May 4, 1945, Washington University held an open house to show off its cyclotron, which was being used for unspecified "scientific research." The $60,000 atom-smashing machine was housed in concrete ten feet underground. It required 150,000 watts of power and was operated by remote control. It was described as "basically a radio oscillator and a magnet," but its function was left unclear. Cyclotron operators had monthly blood tests to check the white blood cell count; nonetheless, the machine was called perfectly safe.

On the morning of August 6, 1945, a uranium ("atomic") bomb was dropped from a B-29 on the city of Hiroshima. The devastation was immediate and far greater than anything even dreamed of before. It was as if two thousand Superforts had each dropped ten tons of TNT at the same time. One hundred thousand people were killed at once, many more died from burns and radiation poisoning in the months ahead. Acres of buildings were ashes. The firestorm following the explosion was so intense that even the river running through the city was in flames.

Soldiers at Scott Field crossed Tokyo off the map when Japan surrendered.

In St. Louis the reaction to the new weapon was much the same as it was across the nation. There was no cheering for the massive destruction, only a hope that it would mean a quick end to the war. E. H. Dillon commented to a *Star-Times* reporter, "This development might obliterate civilization if it isn't controlled. The fear of it, though, may do as much good by restraining nations as its explosive powers do harm."

Although the Hiroshima blast had thrown the Japanese government into havoc, there was no mention of a surrender. On August 9 a plutonium bomb was exploded over Nagasaki. The firestorm it created was visible for 250 miles. It left a crater a mile wide. An editorial predicted that if the A-bomb did not end the war, it would be the "end of humanity."

On August 10 the Japanese offered to surrender, and after four days of negotiating, a surrender agreement was at last reached. The second world war was over.

The next day, August 15, war contracts for area plants totaling $250 million were canceled. On August 16 announcements of layoffs began. Between 65,000 and 85,000 St. Louisans were slated to lose their jobs immediately. At the same time about 150,000 St. Louis servicemen were scheduled to come home. And some 370 price controls, including rent controls, were to be lifted before the end of the month. Like a tea kettle about to whistle, inflation was waiting to explode. It looked like economic chaos ahead.

All summer discharged and furloughed servicemen and women jammed Union Station and downtown hotels as the massive demobilization process began. Eight million people were scheduled to trade uniforms for civvies by the end of 1945. The army set up tem-

St. Louis's Union Station hosted crowds of servicemen and civilians throughout the war.

The demobilization of 1945 strained America's systems of transportation more than anyone thought possible. Americans survived only because they kept a sense of humor. At the St. Louis Women's Advertising Club annual gridiron show, a skit showed a desperate traveler trying to get space on a train bound for Los Angeles. Plaintively she asked, "You mean I can't get ANY space?"

The railroad official replied, "Oh sure, you can get space. What do you want . . . aisle space, standing room on the platform, two feet at the bar, shelf-space in the women's room, or wanta ride the rods?"

porary encampments on the south side and north side of the city with 1,500 beds, and called upon St. Louisans to open their homes to soldiers. All they needed was "a bed, a shower, and a shave" before they went on to their next destination. Kiel Auditorium became a temporary dormitory.

One of those coming through St. Louis on her way home from Europe was war correspondent (for *Colliers*) Martha Gelhorn, daughter of Edna Gelhorn, former suffragist and indefatigable worker for the League of Women Voters. Martha Gelhorn insisted that she was no hero for covering the war. It was "the boys" who had endured boredom, almost continual discomfort, fear, danger, loneliness and dreariness who were the real heroes, she said. (Gelhorn also stated that she would divorce husband Ernest Hemingway soon.)

V-J Day — the war was over at last.

Dancing at the corner of 12th and Olive the night of August 15, 1945.

Among the unsung heroes of the war were the repair units, who had the very unglamorous job of patching up broken machinery, replacing carburetors in jeeps and seeing that half-tracks had the right spark plugs. War correspondent Ernie Pyle wrote,

"This is not a war of ammunition, tanks, guns and trucks alone. It is as much a war of replenishing spare parts to keep them in combat as it is a war of major equipment. . . . The gasket that leaks, the fan belt that breaks, the nut that is lost . . . will delay G. I. Joe."

The African campaign of 1942, which saw scores of trucks, jeeps, and tanks abandoned because they could not be repaired on the spot, led the army to develop an extensive system for maintenance in the field. McCabe Powers Body Company built an ingenious mobile engine shop that could move with the troops and complete major repairs under combat conditions. Herman Body Company developed a similar repair shop for bombers. Carter Carburetor was a major supplier of carburetors for army vehicles; Century Electric and Barrett

The morning after: downtown St. Louis on August 16, 1945.

Electrical Supply produced hydraulic brakes. National Slug Rejectors and Standard Steel Spring Co. made truck axles, and Nixdorff Krein made tow chains for those vehicles that wouldn't start no matter what mechanics did.

Back in February, when Roosevelt was still alive, the "Big Three," FDR, Churchill, and Stalin, met at Yalta to hammer out plans for a lasting peace.

One of the ingredients was a "united nations" organization which would monitor nationalism and aggression throughout the world and thus prevent another world war. During May the fledgling organization met in San Francisco and on June 26, fifty nations signed a world peace charter promising they would make war no more. One of the first decisions the new United Nations organization had to make was where its headquarters would be. The U.S.-U.N. delegate, Edward R. Stettinius (the former secretary of state), suggested that the headquarters be in the center of the nation. He picked out the old ordnance plant at Weldon Spring, Missouri, to be the site. Missouri governor Phil Donnelly, Mayor Kaufmann, and Chamber of Commerce president

Johnny came marching home again, hurrah.

But for the families of those who did not come home, there was only an aching grief. These are reactions to the return of St. Louis war dead.

George Smith lobbyed hard for the honor during the summer of 1945, but finally lost out to New York City. (The Weldon Spring facility was later taken over by Mallinckrodt Chemical Works.)

The end of the war signaled the beginning of a new world. It would have to be a world that worked as hard for peace as it had for war. In late August the army announced that it had sold $3,500,000 worth of equipment at the St. Louis Ordnance plant for scrap. The beating of swords into plowshares had begun.

WINDING DOWN

ON SEPTEMBER 2, 1945, on board the battleship *Missouri* in Tokyo Bay, two representatives of the Japanese government signed the surrender document that made World War II history. It had been less than four years since the attack on Pearl Harbor.

Those four years had affected the American people so profoundly that their impact would be felt for the next four decades. Art, literature, education, science, technology, business, theology, philosophy, politics — all changed because of the war. But probably the greatest changes were social. After the war America began building whole new communities and forging new ways to live.

At the beginning of the war, America was as innocent as the young enlistee who wanted to "beat the Japs" and come home to a happily-ever-after family. The Yanks were underdogs who used bailing wire and string to hold together their single-engine airplanes, who didn't know the difference between a Springfield and a Garand rifle, and who believed, with Superman, in Truth, Justice, and the American Way. At the end, after Bataan and Bastogne and Dachau had lined their faces and hardened their eyes, they found their nation a superpower which had used the deadliest weapon ever known to kill 100,000 people with a single blow. America had a navy and an air force second to none; its intelligence forces had become adept at spying; and the nation became a combatant in a global ideological battle later called the Cold War.

Not even one million of the forty million human beings who died in World War II were Americans, yet the citizens seemed to feel every death as if it were their own and grieved for the suffering of the survivors. From isolationism the country moved to internationalism and opened its pockets and breadbaskets to the world.

At the beginning of the war patriotism was high and no sacrifice seemed too great. Americans were scrappers — no bully was going to get them down. But at the end, it was difficult even to remember to save wastepaper.

In the fall of 1945 St. Louis, like most American communities, did not have time to reflect on what the war had meant. It simply picked up the pieces and went on. For almost fifteen years, through the depression and the war, practically no civic improvements had been made in the city. Civic leaders and businessmen had great hopes for a postwar expansion boom and they painted a glowing picture of a new downtown. Some of their dreams did come true — interstate highways 70, 55, and 44, for instance, and the development of the riverfront into the Jefferson National Expansion Memorial. But most of them did not.

What the city fathers did not foresee or list in their hopeful ''postwar plan'' was the immediate, massive exodus to St. Louis County. The GI Bill gave millions of Americans the opportunity to own their own homes. They wanted new homes with new yards and new futures. Those they could not find in the weather-beaten old city. Almost one hundred suburban communities in St. Louis County welcomed two hundred thousand new residents in the years immediately after the war. And the city never quite recovered from the loss.

Retail stores fled to the suburbs, too, and invented first shopping centers and then malls to bring in customers. Suburban school boards tried to plan for the rapid expansion that the baby boom necessitated, but couldn't keep up with the increasing numbers of new students. Neither could sidewalks, parks, or sewers. The suburban dream generated almost as much anxiety as the urban nightmare.

The suburbs were, practically speaking, all white. In the city, blacks were squeezed into less and less space as urban renewal, or as it was more honestly called, slum clearance, demolished thousands of homes. The war had given impetus to the civil rights movement, but it would be almost twenty years — well after the 1954 Supreme Court decision to end school segregation — before the move for open housing would become strong.

Wartime regulations had seriously hurt small businesses in the area, many of which were forced to close their doors. But the war was a tonic to businesses able to adapt to the pressures of sudden growth and diversification. Some became corporations and then megacorporations with layers of middle management insulating the space between factory and executive suite. The era of shirt-sleeve management was over.

The technological advances that emerged from the war, particularly in medicine and in food preservation, improved the quality of life for all Americans. As soon as consumer goods were again available they were

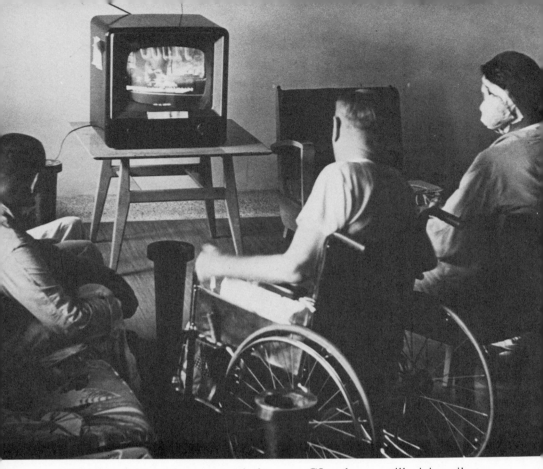

The war didn't end soon enough for some GIs who are still giving silent testimony that there is no such thing as a "good" war.

snapped up with enthusiasm. Everyone wanted new cars, television sets, kitchen appliances, and lawn mowers. Production lines did not slow down, as some economists had predicted, but labor disputes intensified and the gap between labor and management widened.

Most of the returning veterans adapted to civilian life with few problems. Most of the women who had worked in defense production left the line with few regrets and settled in to being fulltime wives and mothers. But in the rush to create a normal family life and an affluent society, Americans — St. Louisans among them — buried their individuality. "Togetherness" and stultifying conformity kept society in bounds until the social explosion of the 1960s.

As the ramifications of World War II were being debated, the men and women who fought in it, produced its bullets and ships, bandaged its wounded and supported its massive bureaucracy, built new lives. Both heroic and cowardly, sacrificial and selfish, they had done what they had to do. No one could ask more.

APPENDIX

St. Louis Firms Contributing to the War Effort
1940-45

AMP Corp. — marine and aircraft products

Absogood Packing Co. "A" — meat for the armed forces

Absorbent Cotton Co. "E" — surgical dressings

Acme Bedding Co.

S.G. Adams — metal mess kits, timing devices for antiaircraft shells, ferrotype plates, engraved instrument panels for aircraft, machine gun mounts

Adams Net & Twine Co. — camouflage nets

Air Reduction Sales Co. "M"

Aircraft Metal Mfg. Co.

Alco Valve Co. "E" control valves for combat planes, hydraulic aircraft controls, radio direction finders on medium and heavy bombers

Alcoa — sheet metal for submarines and aircraft

Alligator Co. — raincoats, coveralls, foul weather gear

Alpha Tank & Metals Mfg. Co.

Alton Box Board Co. "E" — packaging for large bombs

Aluminum Ore Co. [East St. Louis] — ore for Alcoa

Alvey Co. — conveyor assemblies

American Bed & Spring

American Brake Shoe Co. "E"

American Car and Foundry Co. — tanks, hospital cars

American Fixture & Mfg. Co.

American Lithofold Corp. — government forms, comic books for the armed forces

American Optical Co. "E" — aviator sunglasses

American Smelting & Refining Co.

American Steel Foundries [Granite City] "E" — steel for tanks, guns for the navy

American Stove Co. (Magic Chef) — auxiliary gasoline tanks for fighter escorts, 500-lb. general purpose bombs

American Venetian Blind Co.

American Zinc, Lead & Smelting Co. "E" — zinc slabs, cadmium and sulphuric acid for Signal Corps and ordnance department

Amertorp (American Can) "E" — torpedoes

Angelica Corp. — combat uniforms

Anheuser-Busch Co. — food products, subassemblies for gliders, beer for armed forces

Arrow Sportswear — combat jackets

Artcraft Venetian Blind

Atlas Iron Works

Atlas Tool & Mfg. Co.

B-L Electric Mfg. Co. "E"

Baldor Electric Co.

Banner Iron Works, Inc.

Barrett Electrical Supply Co. — brake service equipment

Barry-Wehmiller Co. "E" — sprocket wheels for LVTs, shells, bomber turrets

Baxter-Ramsey Mfg. Co.

Bemis Bag Co. — burlap bags, waterproof bags

Benwood-Linze Co. — Signal Corps equipment

Bierman Iron & Metal Co.

Black Servant Stoker Co. — lugs for bombs

Brauer Supply Co.

Bray Co. — leggings for the army

Braznell Co.

Broderick & Bascom Rope Co. "E" — wire rope for ships, Corps of Engineers

Browning Arms Co.

Buck X-ographic Co. "E" — photographic equipment for the Signal Corps

Brown Shoe Co. — shoes and combat boots for the armed forces

Bugle Metal Products

F. Burkhart Mfg. Co. — mattress pads, bedrolls, cartridge bags for the army

Busch-Sulzer Bros. Diesel Engine Co. "E" — engines for minesweepers and destroyers

Bussmann Co. — electrical equipment, fuses for planes, ships, and tanks

Carondelet Foundry Co.

Carter Carburetor — parts for army jeeps and trucks, bomb and artillery fuses

Centrifugal & Mechanical Industries

Century Electric Co. "E" — hydraulic brakes, parts for army vehicles

Charter Oak Stove & Range Co. — army field ranges, thermal insulators for food storage

Chase Brass & Copper Co., Inc. "E"

Chevrolet/Fisher Body (GM) — DUKWs, 105-mm howitzers

Christopher Aircraft Co.

Chromcraft Mfg. Co. — .30- & .50-caliber ammo boxes; military furniture

Commercial Coffee Co.

Continental Can Co. — tin cases for shipment of .30- and .50-caliber ammunition

G. Cramer Dry Plate Co.

Crown Mfg. Co.

Crunden-Martin Mfg. Co. — helmets, stoves, buckets

Cupples Co. Manufacturers — tire tubes

Curtis Mfg. Co. — refrigeration equipment, compressors

Curtiss-Wright Aircraft Co. — fighter aircraft, cargo planes, trainers

Dazey Mfg. Co. — ammunition fuses and components

Dazor Mfg. Co. — portable lighting fixtures for the army

H. B. Deal & Co. "E"

Defense Plant Corp. — plates and films for the Signal Corps

Diagraph-Bradley — valves and gears for gun turrets and aircraft, stencil equipment

Duke Mfg. Co. — galley equipment for LSTs

Duplex Mfg. Co.

Eberhardt Mfg. Co.

Edison Pipe & Tubing, Inc.

Ehrhardt Tool & Machine "E" — precision gauges

Eisenstadt Mfg. Co.

Elder Mfg. Co. — uniforms for the armed forces

Electric Battery Manufacturers

Emerson Electric Co. "E" — gun turrets for B-17s, B-24s

Empire Stove Co. [Belleville] "E" — bombs, smoke screen tanks for the protection of paratroopers, containers for jelly bombs

Essmueller Co., Inc. — sheet metal, parts for aircraft

Ever Ready Apparel

Export Packing Co. — glider crates, packaging for chemical warfare items

Farmer Mfg. Co.

Federal Barge Line — barges

Fischer Meat Co. — sausage for the army

Flat Steel Mfg. Co.

Flori Pipe Co. — "skegs" for landing craft to protect propeller and rudder

Florissant Fabrication Co.

Forbes Soluable Tea & Coffee Co. — instant coffee for field rations

Foster Bros. Mfg. — steel army cots, berths and fittings for LSTs, aircraft carriers, destroyers, hospitals

Forest City Mfg. Co. — nurses' uniforms

Chester B. Franz Co. "A" — egg and poultry processing for armed forces

George J. Fritz Foundry

Frye Aircraft Co.

Fulton Iron Works Co. — diesel engines, electric generating plants for the USSR

Gardner Metals Co. — parts for gliders

Gaylord Container Corp. (Crown Zellerbach) — packing for bombs

General Cable Corp. "E" — telephone wire for the Signal Corps

General Electric, Lamp Division

General Electric Supplies Co.

General Engineering & Mfg.Co. — machine tools, base plugs for 1,000-pound bomb casings, bomb fin lock nuts, shipshacks for Liberty ships

General Fire Truck Co. — fire fighting equipment for Corps of Engineers

General Metal Products Co. — gauges, tools, precision machined parts

General Refractories Co.

General Steel Castings Corp. — hulls and turrets for M-4 Sherman tanks, T-26 Pershing tanks, gun stands for the navy

Gus Gillerman Iron & Metal Co.

Glidden Paint Co. — paints, varnishes

Grace Sign & Mfg. Co.

Granite City Steel

Gravois Planing Mill

Green Foundry — parts for tanks and trucks, hydraulic brakes

Gruendler Crusher Division — road building equipment for North Africa campaign

W. Grundorf Sheet Metal Works

Guth Lighting — equipment for the Signal Corps, shells and projectiles

Haeter-Koelling Metal Co.

Hager Hinge — hinges and hasps

Hartman Co. — airplane engine starters

Heil Corp. — chemicals, surgical supplies

Heine Boiler Div., Combustion Engr. Co. "M" — boilers for Liberty and Victory ships

Henry Evers Mfg. Co. — tent poles

Herkert & Meisel Trunk Co. — footlockers

Herz Candy Co.

Herman Body Co. — field repair shops for bombers

Highlands Fire Clay Co.

Hunter Packing Co. — food for the army

Hussman-Ligonier "E" — self-contained refrigeration units for the armed forces

Huttig Sash & Door — ammunition boxes

Hydraulic Press Brick Co.

Independent Engineering Co. "E" — high pressure hydrogen generators for Army Air Corps barrage balloons, oxygen cylinders for aircraft, oxygen generators for the South Pacific campaign

International Shoe — combat boots and military shoes, submarine sandals

Jackes-Evans Mfg. Co. "E" — disintegrating links for .30-caliber machine guns

Johansen Bros. Shoe Co. — military shoes, tents

Johnston Tin Foil & Metal Co. "E" — parts for navy anti-aircraft guns

Kearney Electric — electric equipment and switch boxes

Kelvinator — parts for military vehicles

Kilgen Organ Co. — subassemblies for gliders

Kisco Co.

Knapp-Monarch — grenade launchers, VT (proximity) fuses

Koken Companies — glider parts, propellers, bomb casings, examining tables for military medical departments, operating tables for cavalry horses

Koppers Co. — pig iron, benzol, toluol, ammonia

Krey Foods Inc. — K-rations, C-rations for the army

Kroger Co. — food products for the military

Laister-Kauffmann — gliders

Lambert Pharmacal Co. "E" — drugs, medical supplies

Landis Shoe (Sutton-Landis) — machinery for making and repairing shoes; ammunition fuses

Laclede-Christy Clay Products Co. — firebrick and refractory products for steel companies

Lehmann Boring Tool

Leschen Wire Rope Co. — wire rope for Liberty ships

Lever Brothers — soaps and detergents

G. A. Levy & Co.

Lewin Metals Corp. [East St. Louis] — brass shell bands

Lighthouse for the Blind — mops and brooms

Lincoln Engineering Co. "E" — tools for U.S. Cartridge, grease guns for the armed forces, 200-mm explosive shells

Ludlow-Saylor Wire Cloth

McBee Co.

McCabe-Powers Body Co. "E" — truck bodies for army & navy, mobile machine shops for Corps of Engineers, map reproduction railway cars, overland pipe-laying equipment

McDonnell Aircraft Corp. — P-67, experimental jet aircraft, parts for the B-29 Superfortress

McQuay-Norris Industries "E" — bullet cores, artillery fuses, piston rings for aircraft

Madison Ordnance Plant — reclaimed damaged war material

Magnus Metals (National Lead)

Majestic Mfg. Co. "M" — heavy duty ranges for Victory ships

Mallinckrodt, Inc. — photographic chemicals, smokeless powder, burn ointment, fungicide, mercuric oxide for batteries in walkie-talkies, uranium for the atomic bomb

Maloney Electric Co. — transformers and generators for large electrical equipment

W. N. Mathews Corp. "E" — boosters for artillary shells

Mayrose Meatpacking Co. — meat and lard for the armed forces

Measuregraph Co. — 81-mm mortar shells and parts

Medart Mfg. Co. — lockers

Merchants Tire Co.

Mesker Brothers — floats for submarine nets and mines, steel airplane landing mats. accordion doors for hangars, housing for fragmentation bombs, components for floating bridges

Metals Disintegrating Co. — products for the navy

Metal Goods Corp.

Metzger Iron Co. — landing mats

Midwest Piping & Supply "E" — 1,000-lb. demolition bomb casings, fittings for LSTs and LSMs, pipe for destroyers, corvettes, subchasers, cruisers

Mines Equipment Co. "E" — lights for fire control instruments for 155-mm Long Toms

Mississippi Valley Structural Steel "E" — portable bridges

Missouri Jewelite Co.

Missouri Process Sign Co.

Modern Screw Products Co.

Monarch Metal Weatherstrip Co.

Monsanto Chemical Co. "E" — sulfuric acid for TNT, chlorine gas, phenol, nitric acid and fulminate of mercury primers for ammunition, sulfa compounds, drugs

Multiple Boring Machine Co. — lathes, boring machines, drills for shipboard machine shops.

Multiplex Display Co.

Multiplex Faucet Co.

National Bearing Metals Corp. "E" — aluminum, copper, brass, and bronze casings, bearings and babbitt metals

National Bedding Co.

National Carbon Co. — dry batteries for the army and navy

National Enameling & Stamping [Granite City] "E" — Metal containers for gasoline, oil, and water for the armed forces

National Foundry & Machine Co. — bronze and aluminum castings for airplane parts

National Lead Co. [Granite City] — cases for 105-mm shells

National Magnesium Castings Co.

National Slug Rejectors "E" — heavy-duty truck axles, parts for machine guns, parts for aircraft turrets and engines, shell boosters

National Stoker

National Vendors — 75-mm smoke shells

Nestle Company [Granite City] — instant coffee

Nixdorff Krein Industries Inc. — tow chains for the armed forces, "bloomer"chains for paratroopers

Nooter Corp. "E" — tanks for production of penicillin

Northwestern Machine Corp. "E" — fuses for small artillery

Omar Tool & Machine Co.

Orchard Paper Co. — stencils for marking military equipment

Orna-Metal Products Co.

Owens Illinois Glass Co. [Alton] — bombsights, bottles for plasma and drugs

G. H. Packwood Mfg.

Paper Convertors — packing rings for bombs

Peck Products Co. — soap

Perfection Mfg. Co.

L. M. Persons — solenoid and thermostatic controls for bombs

Pet Milk Co. — powdered milk

Pevely Dairy — powdered milk

Phelan-Faust Paint Mfg. Co. — paint

Precision Products — 20-mm armor piercing shells

Premium Cap Co. "E" — army caps

Presstite Engineering Co. — sealants for fuselages, gasoline tanks and other seams in planes, jeeps, and ships

Production Engr. & Mfg.

Progressive Service Co.

Quick Point Pencil Co.

Ralston Purina Co. — supplies for the Quartermaster Corps, K-rations

John Ramming Machine Co. — axles for army trucks

Ramsey Piston Rings Co. — rotating bands, piston rings

Rawlings Sporting Goods Co. "E" — helmets for tank personnel

Reliable Mattress Co.

Rice-Stix Dry Goods Co. "E"

Rite Point Co.

Robertson Aircraft Co. — gliders

Roesch Enamel Range [Belleville] — antiaircraft shells

Rosenthal Paper Co. — boxes for the military

Lee Rowan Co. — arming wires for bombs

Royal Bedding Co.

Royal Packing Co. — beef for the army

S & E Glazer Packing Co. — meat products for the army

St. Louis Aircraft Co. — training planes, high capacity gliders, gondolas for army balloons

St. Louis Car Co. — Water Buffalo amphibious assault craft (LVTs), tanks, electrical generating plants, antenna mounts

St. Louis Cordage Mills

St. Louis Hardware Manufacturing Co.

St. Louis Shipbuilding & Steel Co. — invasion craft, tank barges, towboats, crane barges

St. Louis Silversmiths — precision parts for bombers

St. Louis Steel Casting, Inc.

St. Louis Steel Products — bomb release attachments

St. Louis Screw & Bolt

Sacony-Vacuum — 100-octane aviation fuel

Schaefer Brass & Mfg. Co.

Schlueter Mfg. Co. "E" — army helmets, anti-tank mines

Scullin Steel Co. "E" — earthquake bombs (12,000-lb.) for the RAF, railroad car wheels for portable power plants

Sealtite Corp.

Shapleigh Hardware — tools and

miscellaneous supplies for the armed forces

Shell Oil Co. [Wood River] "E" — 100-octane aviation fuel

W. G. Shelton Co.

Smith & Davis Mfg. Co. — nose struts for B-29s

Society Brand Hat Co. — bell-bottom trousers, gob hats for the navy, officers' caps

Southern Equipment Co. — food service equipment

Southwestern Bell Telephone Co. — training equipment for the Signal Corps, telephone installations for defense plants

Spuck Iron & Foundry

Standard Oil (Indiana) — 100-octane aviation fuel

Standard Steel Spring Co. [Madison, Ill.] — heavy-duty truck axles

Star Mfg. Co.

Sterling Aluminum Products — tools and gauges for U.S. Cartridge, gun turret mounts, aircraft cylinder jackets and pistons

Sterling Steel Castings Co. [Monsanto, Ill.] — steel castings for heavy-duty army transport vehicles, parts for landing craft

Stewart Electric Co. — wiring for defense plants

Stile Craft Manufacturers "E" — bomb parts, shells, ordnance equipment

Stoke-A-Fire Co.

Stout Sign Co.

Stupp Bros. Bridge & Iron Co. "E" — barges, LCTs, Bailey bridges, dry docks

Sunnen Products Co. "E" — precision honing machines and automobile tools

G. S. Suppiger [Belleville] "A" — meat and vegetable hash, meat and vegetable stew, canned chicken for armed forces

Sverdrup & Parcel — airfield design studies, air base and military post design

Tension Envelope Co. — envelopes for military orders, small parts, instruction sheets for tanks, planes, guns

Tobin Electric & Advertising Co.

Tower Grove Foundry

Triple "E" Products Co.

Turner Devices — drafting sets for the GSA

United Drug Co. — drugs and medical supplies

U.S. Cartridge Co. "E" — .30- and .50-caliber cartridges, anti-tank mines

Universal Match Co. "E" — signal flares, magnesium powder

Victory Canvas Co. "E" — canvas field equipment

Wagner Electric Co.

Ely Walker — uniforms, field jackets, pup tents for the army

Walsworth Co. "E" — steel valves and fittings for navy and Merchant Marine ships

Paul K. Weil Co. "E" — helmet liners, parachutes

Weldon Spring Ordnance Plant (Atlas Powder) "E" — TNT for depth charges and blockbuster bombs, DNT, rockets

West St. Louis Machine & Tool

Westcott Valve Co. "E" — valves for the navy

Western Cartridge [East Alton] "E" — smokeless ball powder, ammunition

Western Supplies Co.

Wherry Engineering Co.

Thomas J. White Plastics Co. — molded floors for B-24 Liberators

White-Rogers Electric Co. (Emerson Electric)

Wiles-Chipman Lumber Co. — crates for shipping planes to combat zones

Wright Machinery & Supply Co.

Wrought Iron Range Co. — general purpose bombs, armor piercers and demolition bombs

Zero Mfg. Co.

E = Army-Navy award for excellence
A = Army-Navy award for food suppliers
M = Maritime award

INDEX